# THE INNERVIEW

**EVERYTHING YOU NEED TO KNOW & DO BEFORE YOUR JOB INTERVIEW**

Department of Motivated Vehicles
594 Hancock Street
Suite 3
Brooklyn, NY 11233

# 2. Attract Your D.R.E.A.M. Career

# 3. Build Your D.R.E.A.M. Team 155

# 4. Land Your D.R.E.A.M. Job 189

For the past sixteen years you have been a full-time student, and you have been learning skills and subjects that you hope will prepare you for a career that gives you meaning and money. By now you've probably recognized that you're stronger in some subjects, or at some skills, than you are at others, and that information will inform your career choices. However, while the number of career paths that exists is virtually infinite, the number of classes available in K-12 education and college are not.

Education used to be vocational and prepare you directly for work. The 8a.m.–3 p.m. school day was supposed to prepare you for the 8 a.m–5 p.m. workday. Professors were like your future managers and campuses were like companies. Today that is no longer the case. So, there are two questions at hand:
• How do I figure out what career path is best for me?
• How do I land a job on that career path if college isn't a direct route?
The two answers are the innerview process and the interview process.

**Innerviewing** is an internal process and refers to communication between you and your authentic self. It requires knowing who you are, what you want, and why.

**Interviewing** is an external process and involves an exchange in which two parties interact to get to know each other better. It requires that both the company and the individual interviewee explore what they truly want so that they can determine if there is mutual interest.

Great interviewing is preceded by great innerviewing. Therefore, your discoveries about yourself, your desired career path, and the company (prior to the interview) will be captured in your résumé, cover letter, thirty-second pitch, and interview answers.

Interviewing is natural after you've properly conducted innerviewing, but innerviewing isn't taught anywhere. Instead of self-discovery being a direct result of higher education, it's oftentimes a derivative. The world has shifted drastically and in many ways college hasn't caught up. A good GPA and good personality used to be all you needed to get a good job, but today that isn't the case because a GPA is only a correlative measurement of hard work. In many instances, it measures how much you think within the box rather than how much you think outside of it, which is not an asset when job hunting.

We could have written another standard career exploration textbook for college students that explains the basics of résumés, cover letters, networking, and interviewing, but you can find all of that online. This workbook is designed to prepare you for work. Instead of creating another textbook, we wanted to create a challenging experience, one that helps you to become bigger, better, and bolder and that results in your "Desired Relationship, Employment, and Money" (D.R.E.A.M.).

So, after reviewing all of the top materials on career exploration out there, our goal for this book was four-fold:

1. **Less text:** We've included only materials that are unique, not items that can be found easily online. The easier it is to access information, the more likely it is that

other people are using the same strategies, which ultimately makes you less competitive. You can find more online resources in the appendix.

2. **More exercises:** We call this the **innerviewing** process. Most people skip it and go straight to the interview, but knowing who you are and what you want and don't want is the key to great interviews.

3. **More action:** Each section includes actionable challenges that you can do immediately to move your career exploration process forward.

4. **More results:** Throughout this process you will create your D.R.E.A.M. catchers which include resources such as your cover letter, Résumé 1.0, Résumé 2.0, business cards, website, personal board of directors, and more. Collectively, these deliverables will provide you with everything you need to enhance your interviews and advance your career.

If you do what everyone else does, then you'll get what everyone else gets. We've studied what works and what doesn't work, and we're going to show you how to reroute traditional career tactics (such as copying a résumé template off the Internet and plugging in your information) so that you can distinguish yourself in the job search process.

The challenges laid out in this book are designed to help you succeed personally and professionally. Our hope is that you spend more time in the game and on field than reading about the game from the sidelines. You should be out there meeting new people and new companies, asking thoughtful questions, and trying new things until you find a career that brings out the best in you. Being in the game creates an instant feedback loop that allows you to make changes until you get the result you desire—which in this case is landing your D.R.E.A.M. job before you graduate.

## D.R.E.A.M.

This book is about more than just getting your next job—it's about designing the life you desire, or your version of the American dream. The classic American dream of a nuclear family that goes on trips to Disney Land and has a four-bedroom home and a mini-van and sports car is fading. It's not fading because it is impossible to achieve, but because one size no longer fits all, and each person is starting to define the dream for him/herself.

Dreams are usually considered those ethereal things that you can't touch or ever realize. For us, a dream is not a destination—instead it's a way of being. To be fully alive means to D.R.E.A.M. awake, not day-dream or dream while asleep. What would it look like if you were living your dream every day? Each person must determine his or her individual balance between relationships, employment, and money in order to live the D.R.E.A.M.

**Desired Relationships:** Relationships involve your significant other, children, parents, siblings, extended family, friends, colleagues, and community at large. It also includes your relationship to things that don't involve other people such as yourself, your spiritual source, money, fear, food, trust, love, and so on. We want to ensure that all of your relationships are as healthy as possible.

**Desired Employment:** Employment includes your paid work and **free work** (a.k.a. volunteering). Paid work is likely your full-time job. For most, it involves using their skills to create value forty hours per week. That work can and should be fulfilling—it can and should pay you in intrinsic ways that transcend money. Over half of your waking hours will be at your job, so it's important that your job fulfills you rather than depletes you. Free work involves how you invest your time serving others outside of paid opportunities. This may involve serving in your church, being on the board of a nonprofit, or tutoring youth on evenings or weekends.

**Desired Money:** Money involves your income and assets. How much do you make a month? How much do you keep a month? How much do you have saved? How much do you need to live your D.R.E.A.M. life—do what you want to do and have what you want to have with the person with whom you share your life? Very few people have ever calculated the answer to the question, so they end up playing the profit maximization game; they seek the job that makes them the most money, but it doesn't necessarily make them happy. Keep in mind that your income is not what your employer pays you—that's your revenue. Your income is what you keep after all of your expenses (e.g., rent/mortgage, food, phone, utilities, travel, etc.) are subtracted from your revenues. There are many people who make six-figures in revenue per year from their jobs, but have no income at the end of the year because of their expenses.

For some people, money is everything, and they are willing to work a job they hate and sacrifice their relationships to maximize their financial bottom line. For some people, the job itself is everything, and they will give up income and relationships as long as they are doing what they love. For others, relationships are everything, and it doesn't matter where they work or how much they make as long as they can work with people they care about—colleagues and clients—and afford to be with their loved ones. The trick is that you can't maximize all three. It's like juggling: you need coordination to handle three balls with two hands. Therefore, we each must find our work-life-money balance in order to find our happiness. If you try to copy someone else's balance because of his/her perceived happiness, first know that it's perceived, and two, what's best for others is likely not best for you.

## D.R.E.A.M. JOB

The process we're going to use to explore your D.R.E.A.M. job is organized into the following 4 sections:
1. Create Your D.R.E.A.M. Life (career & life visioning, financial plan).
2. Attract Your D.R.E.A.M. Career (résumé, cover letter, social media, personal branding).
3. Build Your D.R.E.A.M. Team (networking up, across, out, and online).
4. Land Your D.R.E.A.M. Job (job search, interview, follow up, managing up).

**Create Your D.R.E.A.M. Life:** Most people decide on their job first, and then try to build a life around the career. Instead, we're going to begin with your D.R.E.A.M. Life and then find careers that allow you to live your D.R.E.A.M. Life. Most people also define who they are by what they do, when in fact, who you are should define what you do. So in this section we are going to explore your career and life vision using the D.R.E.A.M. framework and then back into career paths that align with your larger vision for your life.

**Attract Your D.R.E.A.M. Career:** Have you ever been attracted to someone? What was it about that person? Was it a combination of features or characteristics that captivated you? How did you even notice him/her? How did you cross paths? You are going to apply the principles of attraction so that you can attract the jobs and employers you want. In this section, we will work on your résumé, cover letter, personal brand, and online presence since these are the tools and mechanisms that employers use to search for those they want to *engage*.

**Build Your D.R.E.A.M. Team:** If you look through your cell phone, it's likely that 95 percent of the people in there are in your peer group (one to three years older or younger than you). They include your friends, colleagues, and acquaintances. The other 5 percent may be older than you, but they include your parents, grandparents, aunts and uncles, and bosses. In order to build a strong D.R.E.A.M. team, you have to network up with mentors, seasoned professionals, and professors. These are the people who can open the doors that you want to knock on because they are already on the other side. Most people spend all of their time networking across to peers, which is good, but networking up is ten times more effective for getting where you want to go. If you're going to ask for directions or help, it's better to ask someone who has already been there, not someone who is right beside you. Here, we will explore how to network up, down, across, out, offline and online so that you can expand the number of people looking out for opportunities that may fit you.

**Land Your D.R.E.A.M. Job:** After you know who you are and what you want, you've accentuated your most attractive features, and someone has made an introduction for you, it's up to you to close the deal. In this section, we will focus on job searching (online and offline), interviewing, following-up, and managing up. You will learn how to access the hidden job market which includes all of the jobs that exist but never get posted on job boards. You will learn what to bring to the interview besides your résumé and how to answer the top twenty interview questions. You will learn how to increase your chances of landing the job through strategic follow-up. Finally, we will discuss how to negotiate your desired income and work style, as well as how to excel in your first three months. Landing your D.R.E.A.M. job is all about showing rather than telling. When you show your results, you take the risk out of hiring for the employer and increase their desire to bring you on board along the way.

## D.R.E.A.M. CATCHERS

In every career exploration process, there will be tools that you develop along the way, and strategies that you use to help you attract and land the job you want. We call them your D.R.E.A.M. catchers. The most common D.R.E.A.M. catchers are your résumé and cover letter, but that's just the beginning. We're going to show you how to create other D.R.E.A.M. catchers that will increase the likelihood of you getting the job you want before graduation.

**Cover Letter:** The purpose of a cover letter is to show the potential employer that you understand the problem (not just the position) they are hiring for and explain why you're the right person for the job. After reading your cover letter, the recipient should be intrigued to learn more about who you are through your résumé.

**Résumé 1.0:** The purpose of your résumé 1.0 is to capture powerful results-based stories from your professional and leadership history in the form of résumé bullets. The ultimate goal of the résumé 1.0 is get you an interview.

**Résumé 2.0:** The purpose of your résumé 2.0 is to be able to show your results, not just tell about them. Its primary use will be in your actual interview. We encourage you to reference it whenever a question posed by the interviewer calls for it. The résumé 2.0 is an opportunity to demonstrate the quality of your work and tell your story in a visual and tactile way.

**Interview Answers:** Your answers to the top twelve interview questions say a lot about your self-awareness and your value. It is possible to anticipate the questions they are going to ask, and thus you put yourself at an advantage if you prepare the strongest answers possible beforehand. If you're innerviewed yourself and researched the company properly, no interview question should be a surprise and your answers should flow naturally.

**Personal Board of Directors:** Most people try to take on the career exploration process alone, but they have a limited awareness about opportunities. A personal board of directors is a team of people who are looking out for your best interests and opportunities that may fit you based on what they know about you. Members can include seasoned professionals, alumni, professors, career counselors, academic advisors, and parents. Whereas peers may be able to point you to the door, your personal board of directors should be in positions that open them.

**Website or Blog:** Almost all companies will Google you before interviewing you, and it is important that you control what they find. You can improve your chances of getting hired by owning your own domain name (www.yourname.com) and having a website or blog that clearly communicates who you are and shows the quality of your thoughts and work. When you put out consistent and quality content on a subject relevant to your career path, potential employers will see your passion, and this will distinguish you from the rest of the pack.

**Facebook & LinkedIn:** Although Facebook seems as if it's a personal space, it's definitely not private. Employers will search for you and look at your pictures and wall. In many ways, how you act in your personal life will carry over into your professional life, and they want to look out for any lewd behavior. LinkedIn, on the other hand, serves as your professional profile online—it's like an online résumé. In addition to allowing you to share your academic achievements and professional pursuits, LinkedIn is perhaps the best research tool for finding insiders you may know in the companies and industries where you want to work.

By the end of this process, you will have all of these D.R.E.A.M. catchers in a place where they are ready for potential employers' eyes. Your personal and professional brand will be consistent across all of your D.R.E.A.M. catchers and employers will get to experience you in a variety of ways beyond the traditional cover letter and résumé 1.0. These extra layers will make all of the difference as you navigate your job or internship search.

## INNERVIEWING

Before you interview, we encourage you to begin by engaging in the innerviewing process. Remember, the innerviewing process is the internal dialogue between you and your best self, whereas the interviewing process is the external dialogue between you and a potential employer.

So many people know what they don't want, but the big question is what do you want?

There are two ways to find the answer—exposure and introspection. If you don't know what you want, don't expect it to come to you naturally. You have to expose yourself to new ideas, new people, new places, and new opportunities. Then, by following whatever interests you, you may stumble upon your passion. Once you discover your passion, deepening it is a never-ending, immersive journey.

Introspection requires sitting with yourself. When you're alone, and your parents, professors, and peers aren't in your head influencing your decision, ask yourself what you really want. Oftentimes, we drive through life under the influence of what others want rather than what we want. So we take the "sexy" jobs at the big name companies because they impress other people. However, the worst thing you can do to yourself is to live a life that makes everyone happy but you.

The innerviewing process involves answering a variety of questions such as:
- What are my passions? What are my interests? What are my hobbies?
- What are my strengths and skills?
- What do I want to be great at professionally?
- What kind of company do I want to work in? Big? Small? Startup? Mature?
- What kind of people do I want to work with?
- What does work-life balance look like to me?
- What is my relationship to work? Is the purpose money, meaning, or both?
- What is my relationship to money? How much is enough? How much is too little?

As you gain clarity on these questions, certain careers will emerge and others will be eliminated because they don't fit your vision for your D.R.E.A.M. Of course, we all want unlimited time, unlimited money, unlimited love, and unlimited passion, but since time is actually a limited resource, we each have to determine how we want to allocate it among our relationships, employment, and pursuit of money. In many cases, a job is the

6

only way people earn income, so the goal becomes to work hard to rise faster. But as you work harder and longer, that time and energy draws from something else you value unless you prioritize properly. Innerviewing will help you make these tough choices ahead of time so that you can find a career path that supports your D.R.E.A.M. life rather than trying to squeeze your D.R.E.A.M. life around your career.

## HOW YOUR COLLEGE CAN HELP YOU D.R.E.A.M.

Today, even a 4.0 GPA isn't enough to guarantee you success personally or professionally. Though important, the world's most successful people didn't have the best GPAs. There are other measurements that correlate with your long-term success better than the GPA alone. The real 4.0 that matters in college is your personal capital, intellectual capital, social capital and financial capital.

**Personal capital** is how well you know yourself. This includes your awareness of your strengths, weaknesses, purpose, passions, and interests. It also has to do with knowing what type of environments, motivators, and people you work well with and which ones you don't. There aren't many classes on college campuses that help you understand who you are, so oftentimes, you have to explore these things outside of class on your own.

**Intellectual capital** is what you know. This includes your expertise in one or two subjects or skills. For some people this is their major, but for most people it's not. When you walk into any room, what subject would feel comfortable speaking on in front of anyone for an hour? Or, what skill can you do well and replicate success more than the average person? So many college graduates graduate with majors and minors, but still lack intellectual capital.

**Social capital** is who you know and who knows you. This includes your networks up, down, across, and out. How many people are listed in your cell phone who aren't family, and who are older than you? Who can you call on when you need professional or personal advice? How many friends can you call on if you need helping moving? How many people are you connected with at different colleges and different organizations across the country? Your social capital can consist of mentors, alumni, seasoned professionals, parents' friends, professors, peers committed to personal greatness, counselors, coaches, and advisors, among others.

**Financial capital** is who knows that you know what you know---that's a tricky one. When the right people know that you know a lot about a subject, or can execute a skill that they need, that's when financial opportunities flow. It's a combination of your intellectual and social capital. The interview process is all about building a relationship with the hiring manager, interviewers, and the company, and then convincing them that you are the most knowledgeable and skillful at solving the problem they are hiring for. Anyone who knows people in a desirable company has an advantage because referrals are one of the top ways people get jobs. Also, those who can show through past performance that they are the best at what they do will have an advantage in the hiring process as well.

Your campus has intellectual, social, and financial capital, too. So, you want to use its capital to develop yours—that's what your four years are about. You want to graduate as a more valuable commodity than you were when you started college. Graduation and a good GPA by themselves don't guarantee that you're more valuable to potential employers.

Your campus' intellectual capital includes classes, professors, guest lecturers, online databases, libraries, departments, centers, and specialized offices. The more you are aware of which resources are relevant to where you want to go, the better off you will be upon graduation.

Your campus' social capital includes professors, older alumni, recent alumni, faculty and staff. The stronger your relationships are with key people on campus, the more likely it is that opportunities will find you because these people are the ones who either offer the opportunities or learn about the opportunities first.

Your campus' financial capital includes financial aid, student government, and scholarships, as well as your access to resources, information, and equipment that most people would have to pay for (e.g., online databases, video cameras, etc.). You can find scholarships on-campus just by knowing the right people, and you can access resources that save you money.

In regards to your career exploration process, explore classes, offices, and student groups that can help you develop your personal, intellectual, social, and financial capital before you graduate.

# 1. CREATE YOUR D.R.E.A.M. LIFE

## 2. ATTRACT YOUR D.R.E.A.M. CAREER

## 3. BUILD YOUR D.R.E.A.M. TEAM

## 4. LAND YOUR D.R.E.A.M. JOB

# HOW TO D.R.E.A.M. AGAIN

As expressed in the introduction, to **D.R.E.A.M.** means to have your Desired Relationships, Employment, And Money. When we think about our dreams, we tend to think about a destination—perhaps retired on a beach with your significant other—as opposed to the joy of a journey that could one day get us there.

You will spend more time at your job than with your spouse between the ages of twenty-five and sixty-five, which means that it is important that you are happy at work. Consequently, the goal of many people is early retirement simply because they hate their jobs and want to move on to something better. However, according to Gallup, the average retirement age of people who live beyond ninety years is eighty. Of these late retirees, 93 percent of them got great satisfaction from their careers, and 83 percent had fun working. It's easy to envision life after work, but we rarely envision our perfect average day.

Your time is your most valuable resource and how you allocate it will determine the quality of your life. By beginning with your perfect average day—a day you would be happy to experience over and over and over again, we can begin exploring any alignment or misalignment that exists in your D.R.E.A.M. Is it possible to be a CEO of a global company and still attend all of your kids' baseball games and recitals? Is it possible to have that big house and vacation home given the average salary for the career path you want to pursue?

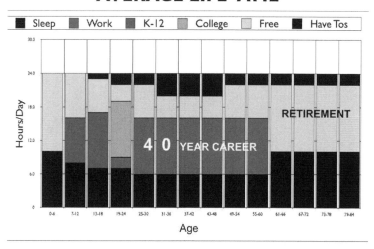

In this section we want to make your D.R.E.A.M. as real as possible. However, rather than defining what titles you want to have and what things you want to have years from now, we're going to start by defining what you want to do on your perfect average day. One of the goals, then, is to find enjoyment in the many moments of life rather than occasional, temporary happiness. You should look for your joy first and your job second.

We each get a 168 hour cup to fill every week. Some people let life fill up the cup first and then try to pour in time for themselves afterwards. Others pour in time for what they want first and then let life fill up the rest. Either way, you get to choose. We all have a D.R.E.A.M., and now is your chance to define it for yourself.

## PERFECT AVERAGE DAY

**Directions:** Dream about what your perfect average day would be like and write it down hour by hour.

**06:00AM**...................................................................................................

**07:00AM**...................................................................................................

**08:00AM**...................................................................................................

**09:00AM**...................................................................................................

**10:00AM**...................................................................................................

**11:00AM**...................................................................................................

**12:00PM**...................................................................................................

**01:00PM**...................................................................................................

**02:00PM**...................................................................................................

**03:00PM**...................................................................................................

**04:00PM**...................................................................................................

**05:00PM**...................................................................................................

## OTHER NOTES:

...................................................................................................

...................................................................................................

...................................................................................................

...................................................................................................

...................................................................................................

...................................................................................................

...................................................................................................

**PERFECT AVERAGE DAY CONTINUED...**

**Directions:** Dream about what your perfect average day would be like and write it down hour by hour.

**06:00PM**......................................................................................................................

**07:00PM**......................................................................................................................

**08:00PM**......................................................................................................................

**09:00PM**......................................................................................................................

**10:00PM**......................................................................................................................

**11:00PM**......................................................................................................................

**12:00AM**......................................................................................................................

**01:00AM**......................................................................................................................

**02:00AM**......................................................................................................................

**03:00AM**......................................................................................................................

**04:00AM**......................................................................................................................

**05:00AM**......................................................................................................................

**OTHER NOTES:**

..........................................................................................................................

..........................................................................................................................

..........................................................................................................................

..........................................................................................................................

..........................................................................................................................

..........................................................................................................................

..........................................................................................................................

..........................................................................................................................

## DESIRED RELATIONSHIPS

**Directions:** Dream about how you want your relationships to be and write it down.

**My spouse and I**...................................................................................................................

...................................................................................................................

...................................................................................................................

**My children and I**...................................................................................................................

...................................................................................................................

...................................................................................................................

**My parent/s and I**...................................................................................................................

...................................................................................................................

...................................................................................................................

**My friends and I**...................................................................................................................

...................................................................................................................

...................................................................................................................

**My colleagues and I**...................................................................................................................

...................................................................................................................

...................................................................................................................

**My siblings and I**...................................................................................................................

...................................................................................................................

...................................................................................................................

**My**...................... **and I**...................................................................................................................

...................................................................................................................

...................................................................................................................

## DESIRED EMPLOYMENT

**Directions:** Dream about how you want your employment to be and write it down.

**In my eyes, the purpose of work is**..................................................................

..........................................................................................................................

**I want to evaluate my career every**.............**years.**

**I want to work in** ❑ **for-profit** ❑ **nonprofit** ❑ **government** ❑ **a combination.**

**I want to work for** ❑ **a big company** ❑ **a small company** ❑ **a startup** ❑ **myself.**

**I want to work a maximum of** ❑ **40 hrs/week** ❑ **60 hrs/week** ❑ **80+ hrs/week.**

**I want to work for a company that** ..................................................................

..........................................................................................................................

..........................................................................................................................

**I want to be in a work environment that** .......................................................

..........................................................................................................................

..........................................................................................................................

**I want to work in a position that** ....................................................................

..........................................................................................................................

..........................................................................................................................

**I want to work with colleagues who** .............................................................

..........................................................................................................................

..........................................................................................................................

**I expect my work and employer to**.................................................................

..........................................................................................................................

..........................................................................................................................

**DESIRED MONEY**

**Directions:** Dream about how much money you want and how you will allocate it.

*INCOME*
**My mom made............................ per year. My dad made............................ per year.**

**I would be ☐ dissatisfied ☐ comfortable ☐ happy ☐ very happy with their earnings.**

**Enough income would be $......................Too much would be $....................................**

**I want to give ............% of my income to good causes (e.g., charities, church).**

**I intend to create $ .......................... in passive income annually by...........................**

**...........................................................................................................................**

*SAVINGS*
**I want to save ..................% of my income.**

**I want to retire by the age of......................with a savings of.....................................**

**I intend to pay......................% of my children's college loans.**

**I will buy a house when I've saved.......................... and/or have ...................income.**

**I will buy a car when I've saved............................ and/or have .......................income.**

*EXPENSES*
**The features of the house I want include..................................................................**

**...........................................................................................................................**

**I want to buy my first house by the age of...............................................................**

**The kind/s of car/s I want include............................................................................**

**Some of the luxury items I want include...................................................................**

**...........................................................................................................................**

**I want to go on ......... personal vacations and ......... family vacations every 4 years.**

**Other major lifestyle expenses include....................................................................**

**...........................................................................................................................**

# 1.2 HOW TO CALCULATE YOUR FINANCIAL FREEDOM

Financial freedom is the goal of a lot of people. Nonetheless, it's not financial freedom that people really want; rather, they really want the freedom to do what they want, when they want to do it. This doesn't mean relaxing and doing nothing all day. What we really want is the opportunity to spend our time in a way that contributes to both others and ourselves simultaneously.

When people say they want to be rich, they rarely have a specific financial number that defines rich for them. In America, we have an infatuation with becoming a millionaire, but financial freedom is not about income maximization, it's about lifestyle design in relationship to income. Most people underestimate how much they actually spend every month, and they overestimate how much they need to be happy. When they are unsure, the safest path is income maximization which means taking the job that pays the most even if you hate it.

In this section we're going to explore how financially free you are by calculating your **runway**—the number of months you could pay your monthly expenses out of your current assets if you stopped generating income today. As college students your runway may be short because you may not be working and are solely dependent on financial aid or parents, or you work a part-time job that doesn't pay much.

As you step into your career, that will change, but if your cost of living increases faster that your increase in income, you will find that, even with a job, your runway is still short. There are people who make over $100,000 per year, but have short runways because they bought a house, car, and other things that increase their cost of living to the same amount as their income. The secret to financial well being is to live simply by living below your means without sacrificing your comfort. Each of us has to define what is "enough" and then live without comparing ourselves to others.

This following exercise may not be relevant at this time of your life, but it will prepare you for the real world. According to Gallup, 44 percent of employees say they could go only a month after losing their job before experiencing significant financial hardship, and another 27 percent say they could last up to four months. Some of you may need to take a **bridge job**—a job opportunity that serves as a bridge between where you are and your D.R.E.A.M. job that will develop your personal, intellectual, social, or financial capital—after graduation just to get settled into the real world. But if you know the industry you want to be in and its **profit margin**—the percentage a company keeps in profit on every dollar of revenue—you will know how much value you need to be able to prove you can create to a potential employer to get the job and income you want.

## MONTHLY EXPENSES & ASSETS

**Directions:** Grab a calculator, recent monthly bills, and your last few bank statements. Complete and calculate all of your monthly expenses. Calculate your runway by dividing Total Assets by Total Monthly Expenses.

### EXAMPLE MONTHLY EXPENSES

| Line Item | Monthly Expenses | Examples |
|---|---|---|
| Rent/Mortgage | $700 | |
| Utilities | $100 | gas, water, power |
| Phones | $200 | home, cell |
| House Stuff | $50 | Internet, TV, supplies |
| Insurance | $60 | health, home, car, etc |
| Entertainment | $150 | movies, parties, etc |
| Food | $300 | groceries, dining, etc |
| Automobile | $389 | gas, maintenance, parking |
| Loans & Credit Cards | $510 | student loans, etc |
| Other #1: | | |
| Other #2: | | **Minimum Annual Salary** |
| **Total Monthly Expenses** | $2459 | x 12 = $29,508 |

### EXAMPLE ASSETS

| Source | Amount |
|---|---|
| Checking Account | $5400 |
| Savings Account | $9000 |
| Other #1: | |
| Other #2: | |
| **Total Assets** | $14400 |

**MY CURRENT MONTHLY EXPENSES**

| Line Item | Monthly Expenses | Examples |
|---|---|---|
| Rent/Mortgage | | |
| Utilities | | gas, water, power |
| Phones | | home, cell |
| House Stuff | | internet, TV, supplies |
| Insurance | | health, home, car, etc |
| Entertainment | | movies, parties, etc |
| Food | | groceries, dining, etc |
| Automobile | | gas, maintenance, parking |
| Loans & Credit Cards | | student loans, etc |
| Other #1: | | |
| Other #2: | | **Minimum Annual Salary** |
| **Total Monthly Expenses** | | x 12 = |

**MY CURRENT ASSETS**

| Source | Amount |
|---|---|
| Checking Account | |
| Savings Account | |
| Other #1: | |
| Other #2: | |
| **Total Assets** | |

Divide **Total Assets** by **Total Monthly Expense**.

If I graduated today, I would have a

$$=\$ \frac{14{,}000}{\$ \quad 2{,}459}$$

= **5.8** month runway.

In order to save or invest half of my income each month, I need to earn two times my current monthly expenses which is

= $ **4,918** per month

x 12 months

= $ **59,016** per year

Considering that the profit margin in my industry in my desired industry is

(Visit http://biz.yahoo.com/p/sum_qpmd.html to find the profit margin.)

= **25** %

I need to prove to my future employer that I can create at least

$$\$ \frac{59{,}016}{100\% - 25\%} = \$ \frac{59{,}016}{0.75} =$$

= $ **78,688** in value (i.e., revenue) per year or else it doesn't make sense for them to hire me.

| Industry | Profit Margin |
|---|---|
| 1 Beverages - Brewers | 25.9% |
| 2 Closed-End Fund - Debt | 25.3 |
| 3 REIT - Healthcare Facilities | 24.6 |
| 4 Application Software | 22.7 |
| 5 Information & Delivery Services | 17.8 |
| 6 Cigarettes | 17.4 |
| 7 Drug Manufacturers - Major | 16.5 |
| 8 Networking & Communication Device | 16.3 |
| 9 Agricultural Chemicals | 15.2 |
| 10 Industrial Metals & Minerals | 14.8 |
| 11 REIT - Residential | 13.8 |
| 12 Security Software & Services | 13.5 |
| 13 REIT - Retail | 13.5 |
| 14 Drug Delivery | 13.5 |
| 15 Railroads | 12.9 |
| 16 Gas Utilities | 12.6 |
| 17 Personal Products | 12.3 |
| 18 Beverages - Wineries & Distillers | 11.8 |
| 19 Education & Training Services | 11.7 |
| 20 Diversified Communication Services | 11.7 |
| 21 Wireless Communications | 11.1 |
| 22 Personal Services | 10 |
| 23 Oil & Gas Drilling & Exploration | 9.7 |
| 24 Healthcare Information Services | 9.3 |
| 25 Air Services, Other | 9.2 |
| 26 Processed & Packaged Goods | 9 |
| 27 Telecom Services - Domestic | 8.9 |
| 28 Diversified Computer Systems | 8.9 |
| 29 Diversified Utilities | 8.8 |
| 30 Home Health Care | 8.4 |
| 31 Oil & Gas Equipment & Services | 8.3 |
| 32 Medical Laboratories & Research | 8.2 |
| 33 Business Software & Services | 8 |
| 34 Restaurants | 7.5 |
| 35 Personal Computers | 7.5 |
| 36 Food - Major Diversified | 7.4 |
| 37 Foreign Regional Banks | 7.3 |
| 38 Publishing - Books | 7.1 |
| 39 Cleaning Products | 7.1 |
| 40 Regional - Northeast Banks | 7 |
| 41 Medical Instruments & Supplies | 6.8 |
| 42 General Entertainment | 6.8 |
| 43 Conglomerates | 6.7 |
| 44 Biotechnology | 6.7 |
| 45 Drugs - Generic | 6.6 |
| 46 Textile - Apparel Footwear | 6.4 |
| 47 Internet Information Providers | 6.2 |
| 48 Telecom Services - Foreign | 6.1 |
| 49 Electric Utilities | 6.1 |
| 50 Sporting Activities | 6 |
| 51 Research Services | 5.8 |
| 52 Pollution & Treatment Controls | 5.8 |
| 53 Auto Parts Stores | 5.8 |
| 54 Beverages - Soft Drinks | 5.7 |
| 55 Waste Management | 5.6 |
| 56 Business Services | 5.5 |
| 57 Small Tools & Accessories | 5.3 |
| 58 Regional - Southwest Banks | 5.3 |
| 59 Publishing - Periodicals | 5.2 |
| 60 Aerospace Products & Services | 5.2 |
| 61 Processing Systems & Products | 5 |
| 62 Tobacco Products, Other | 4.8 |
| 63 Metal Fabrication | 4.8 |
| 64 Management Services | 4.8 |
| 65 Recreational Vehicles | 4.7 |
| 66 Aerospace Major Diversified | 4.7 |
| 67 Oil & Gas Pipelines | 4.6 |
| 68 Recreational Goods, Other | 4.4 |
| 69 Information Technology Services | 4.3 |
| 70 Consumer Services | 4.3 |
| 71 Specialty Eateries | 4.1 |
| 72 Auto Parts Wholesale | 4 |
| 73 Accident & Health Insurance | 3.8 |
| 74 Nonmetallic Mineral Mining | 3.6 |
| 75 Insurance Brokers | 3.6 |
| 76 Industrial Equipment & Components | 3.6 |
| 77 **Hospitals** | **3.6** |
| 78 Electronics Stores | 3.6 |
| 79 Oil & Gas Refining & Marketing | 3.5 |
| 80 Major Integrated Oil & Gas | 3.5 |
| 81 Industrial Electrical Equipment | 3.5 |
| 82 Data Storage Devices | 3.5 |
| 83 Confectioners | 3.5 |
| 84 Home Furnishing Stores | 3.3 |
| 85 Heavy Construction | 3.3 |
| 86 **Health Care Plans** | **3.3** |

Divide **Total Assets** by **Total Monthly Expense**.

If I graduated today, I would have a

=$_____
  $

= _____ month runway.

In order to save or invest half of my income each month, I need to earn 2 times my current monthly expenses which is

= $_____ per month

x 12 months

= $_____ per year

Considering that the profit margin in my industry in my desired industry is

(Visit http://biz.yahoo.com/p/sum_qpmd.html to find the profit margin.)

= _____ %

I need to prove to my future employer that I can create at least

$_____ = $_____ =

= $_____ in value (i.e., revenue) per year
or else it doesn't make sense for them to hire me.

| Industry | Profit Margin |
|---|---|
| 1 Beverages - Brewers | 25.9% |
| 2 Closed-End Fund - Debt | 25.3 |
| 3 REIT - Healthcare Facilities | 24.6 |
| 4 Application Software | 22.7 |
| 5 Information & Delivery Services | 17.8 |
| 6 Cigarettes | 17.4 |
| 7 Drug Manufacturers - Major | 16.5 |
| 8 Networking & Communication Device | 16.3 |
| 9 Agricultural Chemicals | 15.2 |
| 10 Industrial Metals & Minerals | 14.8 |
| 11 REIT - Residential | 13.8 |
| 12 Security Software & Services | 13.5 |
| 13 REIT - Retail | 13.5 |
| 14 Drug Delivery | 13.5 |
| 15 Railroads | 12.9 |
| 16 Gas Utilities | 12.6 |
| 17 Personal Products | 12.3 |
| 18 Beverages - Wineries & Distillers | 11.8 |
| 19 Education & Training Services | 11.7 |
| 20 Diversified Communication Services | 11.7 |
| 21 Wireless Communications | 11.1 |
| 22 Personal Services | 10 |
| 23 Oil & Gas Drilling & Exploration | 9.7 |
| 24 Healthcare Information Services | 9.3 |
| 25 Air Services, Other | 9.2 |
| 26 Processed & Packaged Goods | 9 |
| 27 Telecom Services - Domestic | 8.9 |
| 28 Diversified Computer Systems | 8.9 |
| 29 Diversified Utilities | 8.8 |
| 30 Home Health Care | 8.4 |
| 31 Oil & Gas Equipment & Services | 8.3 |
| 32 Medical Laboratories & Research | 8.2 |
| 33 Business Software & Services | 8 |
| 34 Restaurants | 7.5 |
| 35 Personal Computers | 7.5 |
| 36 Food - Major Diversified | 7.4 |
| 37 Foreign Regional Banks | 7.3 |
| 38 Publishing - Books | 7.1 |
| 39 Cleaning Products | 7.1 |
| 40 Regional - Northeast Banks | 7 |
| 41 Medical Instruments & Supplies | 6.8 |
| 42 General Entertainment | 6.8 |
| 43 Conglomerates | 6.7 |
| 44 Biotechnology | 6.7 |
| 45 Drugs - Generic | 6.6 |
| 46 Textile - Apparel Footwear | 6.4 |
| 47 Internet Information Providers | 6.2 |
| 48 Telecom Services - Foreign | 6.1 |
| 49 Electric Utilities | 6.1 |
| 50 Sporting Activities | 6 |
| 51 Research Services | 5.8 |
| 52 Pollution & Treatment Controls | 5.8 |
| 53 Auto Parts Stores | 5.8 |
| 54 Beverages - Soft Drinks | 5.7 |
| 55 Waste Management | 5.6 |
| 56 Business Services | 5.5 |
| 57 Small Tools & Accessories | 5.3 |
| 58 Regional - Southwest Banks | 5.3 |
| 59 Publishing - Periodicals | 5.2 |
| 60 Aerospace Products & Services | 5.2 |
| 61 Processing Systems & Products | 5 |
| 62 Tobacco Products, Other | 4.8 |
| 63 Metal Fabrication | 4.8 |
| 64 Management Services | 4.8 |
| 65 Recreational Vehicles | 4.7 |
| 66 Aerospace Major Diversified | 4.7 |
| 67 Oil & Gas Pipelines | 4.6 |
| 68 Recreational Goods, Other | 4.4 |
| 69 Information Technology Services | 4.3 |
| 70 Consumer Services | 4.3 |
| 71 Specialty Eateries | 4.1 |
| 72 Auto Parts Wholesale | 4 |
| 73 Accident & Health Insurance | 3.8 |
| 74 Nonmetallic Mineral Mining | 3.6 |
| 75 Insurance Brokers | 3.6 |
| 76 Industrial Equipment & Components | 3.6 |
| 77 **Hospitals** | **3.6** |
| 78 Electronics Stores | 3.6 |
| 79 Oil & Gas Refining & Marketing | 3.5 |
| 80 Major Integrated Oil & Gas | 3.5 |
| 81 Industrial Electrical Equipment | 3.5 |
| 82 Data Storage Devices | 3.5 |
| 83 Confectioners | 3.5 |
| 84 Home Furnishing Stores | 3.3 |
| 85 Heavy Construction | 3.3 |
| 86 **Health Care Plans** | **3.3** |

# 1.3 HOW TO BUDGET FOR YOUR CAREER DISCOVERY

One of the greatest barriers to career discovery is the hidden cost of time and money. Just like applying to college or graduate school, you should plan up front. For college you had to do research, study for tests, take tests, do campus visits, and complete essays and applications. However, at that time you were likely doing it on your parents' dime and time.

With career discovery, you will also have to conduct research, go through multiple interview processes, sometimes travel, and complete applications. The only real difference is that you have to make the time, and you may have to pay by yourself. Career discovery is an investment in your future, and getting this answer right early on is priceless.

One of the most valuable parts of your career discovery process will be other people. It takes time and money to cultivate real relationships. So, you need to budget for quick coffees with alumni, lunches with professors, and dinners with mentors. (Mentors don't usually make you pay, but just in case.) After meeting with any of these people, you should send a thank you card, so you will need to buy cards and postage.

For your interviews, you will need a few business suits, shirts/ blouses, shoes, and other accessories. These items can get expensive if you don't already have them. You may also want to buy a padfolio to hold copies of your résumé printed on premium résumé paper. We also encourage you to buy business cards to show your professionalism when interviewing and for networking purposes.

Finally, there are professional organizations that you may want to join that require annual membership fees. In addition, there may be tests or certifications that you want to take in advance to show your competence and initiative.

## CAREER DISCOVERY BUDGET

**Directions:** Determine what combination of items you're willing to invest in for your career discovery process.

**SAMPLE BASIC BUDGET**

| Line Item | Cost/Each | # of Each | Total Cost |
|---|---|---|---|
| *Example: Lunches* | *$30* | *3* | *$90* |
| Coffees | $10 | | |
| Lunches | $30 | | |
| Dinners | $50 | | |
| Thank You Cards & Postage | $2 | | |
| Padfolio | $25 | | |
| Business Cards | $20 | | |
| Domain Name | $10 | | |
| Books to Buy | $20 | | |
| Printing | $50 | | |
| **Total Basic Budget** | | | |

**SAMPLE BIG BUDGET**

| Line Item | Cost/Each | # of Each | Total Cost |
|---|---|---|---|
| Membership | $300 | | |
| Conferences | $500 | | |
| Certification Test | $150 | | |
| Test Prep Course | $500 | | |
| Other #1: | | | |
| Other #2: | | | |
| **Total Big Budget** | | | |

Since discovering my D.R.E.A.M. job would be priceless, I am willing to set aside a budget of $_____ for my career discovery process.

# 1.4 A  HOW TO CALCULATE YOUR CURRENT PROFESSIONAL VELOCITY

You remember the concept of velocity from physics: change in distance over change in time. The reason we are willing to pay more for an airplane ticket for long distance travel than we are for a train, bus, or car is that it can close the distance between where we are (Point A) and where we want to be (Point B) faster, safer, and easier than the other forms of transportation. The same principle applies for your career.

**Professional velocity** is the rate at which you can help other organizations or individuals get from a Point A to a Point B. It is highly correlative with your income.

Here's an example of professional velocity. Let's say that someone wants to get in shape and lose 50 pounds. The person currently weighs 250 pounds (Point A) and wants to get to 200 pounds (Point B) in 6 months. He or she has been trying on his/her own, but the dieting and gym haven't been working. So a personal trainer comes in and says, "I can help you get from 250 pounds to 200 pounds in 4 months, guaranteed. and my rate is $50 per hour. If the person really wants to reach the goal of 200 pounds and is convinced by the personal trainer's past results that s/he can help the dieter to achieve the goal faster, safer, and easier than in a solo effort, then the personal trainer's professional velocity is $50 per hour.

Imagine that you're working a part-time job while being a full-time student, and you get paid $25 per hour. When you extend that at 40 hours per week for 50 weeks per year, that's $50,000 per year. But when you break down your professional velocity per minute, you're only being paid for creating $0.33 of value per minute for your company. which doesn't sound like a lot. However, if you can create more, you can earn more.

Professional velocity can only be determined by past performance. That's why college is so important. It creates a safe four-year space and time for you to perform and show the world what you're made of. College is like a microcosm of the world, and if you prove you can excel here, then you can make a more believable argument about your ability to excel in the world at large during your interview process. Then you can claim the professional velocity you deserve. Your grades are only part of your professional velocity. You must also consider your leadership, your awards, your extracurricular activities, your personal projects, your internships, and other experiences that demonstrate your ability to deliver great work. This is how you differentiate yourself in the eyes of potential employers.

**YOUR CURRENT PROFESSIONAL VELOCITY**

YOUR CURRENT HOURLY RATE $ **25** x 8 HOURS x 250 DAYS =

YOUR CURRENT ANNUAL SALARY = $ **50,000**

52 WEEKS - **2** VACATION WEEKS = **50** **WEEKS**

= $ **1,000** **PER WEEK**

DIVIDED BY AVERAGE HOURS PER WEEK

**50** **HOURS PER WEEK**
Includes travel to and from work

= $ **20** **PER HOUR**

DIVIDED BY 60 MINUTES

= $ **0.33** **PER MINUTE**

DIVIDED BY 60 SECONDS

= $ **0.0055** **PER SECOND**

NOTE: This only assumes income generated from your job. It does not account for passive income from other assets such as real estate, stocks, or mutual funds.

**YOUR CURRENT PROFESSIONAL VELOCITY**

**Directions:** Complete the worksheet below based on the previous example to calculate your current professional velocity.

YOUR CURRENT ANNUAL SALARY = **$**
_____

52 WEEKS - _____ VACATION WEEKS =        **WEEKS**

= $_____ **PER WEEK**

DIVIDED BY AVERAGE HOURS PER WEEK

_____ **HOURS PER WEEK**
Includes travel to and from work

= $_____ **PER HOUR**

DIVIDED BY 60 MINUTES

= $_____ **PER MINUTE**

DIVIDED BY 60 SECONDS

= $_____ **PER SECOND**

NOTE: This only assumes income generated from your job. It does not account for passive income from other assets such as real estate, stocks, or mutual funds.

# 1.4 B  HOW TO CALCULATE YOUR DESIRED PROFESSIONAL VELOCITY

In our last example, you were being paid for creating 33 cents of value for your employer every minute. Now imagine if you could figure out a way to be more valuable and create $1.00 in value per minute for your current company, another company, or your own company. You could triple your annual salary.

Your time is your greatest asset. In the **Average Business Cycle (See Module 2.9)**— how a company uses its resources to make money—human capital or time is the hardest thing to manage. In the same way, our own time management can be poor. However, if you ask yourself, "What's the best way to invest my forty hours this week that will create the most value?" you will find that it likely doesn't involve doing what you're currently doing. It probably involves less e-mail, fewer meetings, and a shorter to-do list. Instead, it will require laser focus on one or two items that could radically change everything if, or when, it works.

Using your time more effectively means that you may not have to work a nine-to-five job. You may not have to work fifty weeks per year. You may not have to work at all. You can start breaking some of the myths and assumptions people have about work when you learn to invest your time wisely. Harder work and more work don't necessarily guarantee greater results.

If you're still thinking about financial freedom, follow this calculation. If you divide $50,000 dollars by the number of minutes in a year, which is 547,500 minutes (= 365 days x 24 hours/day x 60 minutes/hour), that equals nine cents per minute. What that means is that if you could get the world to put nine cents in your pocket every minute, even when you were asleep, you could earn just as much as you do working for someone else 40-50 hours per week.

A good question to consider is "How much would I pay myself if I had to hire myself?" We are comfortable throwing out big numbers when it isn't our money, but honestly, how much do you think you're worth? The reality is that you're not worth anything professionally until you prove you are, so your early career should be focused on developing proof points so that you can achieve your desired professional velocity sooner than later.

In this section, determine your desired annual salary and number of vacation weeks. Your vacation days don't have to add up to only two weeks. Also, determine how many hours you want to work per week. See how that changes your professional velocity so that you focus on developing proof points that match what you desire.

**SAMPLE PROFESSIONAL VELOCITY CALCULATION**

YOUR DESIRED ANNUAL SALARY = $ **200,000**

52 WEEKS - **12** VACATION WEEKS = **40** **WEEKS**

= $ **5,000** **PER WEEK**

DIVIDED BY AVERAGE HOURS PER WEEK

**50** **HOURS PER WEEK**
Includes travel to and from work

= $ **100** **PER HOUR**

DIVIDED BY 60 MINUTES

= $ **1.67** **PER MINUTE**

DIVIDED BY 60 SECONDS

= $ **0.03** **PER SECOND**

NOTE: This only assumes income generated from your job. It does not account for passive income from other assets such as real estate, stocks, or mutual funds.

**YOUR DESIRED PROFESSIONAL VELOCITY**

**Directions:** Complete the worksheet below based on the previous example to calculate your desired professional velocity.

YOUR DESIRED ANNUAL SALARY = **$**

_____

52 WEEKS - _____ VACATION WEEKS = **WEEKS**

**= $**_____ **PER WEEK**

DIVIDED BY AVERAGE HOURS PER WEEK

_____ **HOURS PER WEEK**
Includes travel to and from work

**= $**_____ **PER HOUR**

DIVIDED BY 60 MINUTES

**= $**_____ **PER MINUTE**

DIVIDED BY 60 SECONDS

**= $**_____ **PER SECOND**

NOTE: This only assumes income generated from your job. It does not account for passive income from other assets such as real estate, stocks, or mutual funds.

# 1.5 HOW TO CREATE YOUR PERSONAL SUCCESS DASHBOARD

Imagine driving a car without a dashboard. Consider all of the things that could go wrong simply by not having a way to measure how fast, how far, how full, and how hot the car is. You wouldn't know if you were above the speed limit and could therefore get speeding tickets. You wouldn't know when your engine needs oil or is overheating. You wouldn't know when you need to fill up your tank with gas until it just gives out on you. You wouldn't know when to take your car in for scheduled maintenance and thus could cause major damage to expensive parts. In the same way, it's important for you to create measurements for your success—even if some of them are only correlative—so that you don't risk not knowing and comparing your success to those around you.

Society's default dashboard for success includes money, power, beauty, and fame. Until you consciously create your own dashboard for success, you will simply adopt society's default dashboard, or your parents' dashboard for success. But the definition of success changes from one generation to the next, so it's unlikely that what worked for your parents and made them happy will work exactly the same for you. That's why it is important to define success for yourself and pursue it on your own terms.

In this section, you get the opportunity to create a dashboard for yourself, personally and professionally. You shouldn't consult anyone on this exercise. The answers should come straight from you. There are so many ways to define and measure success beyond money, power, beauty, and fame. One or two of those may be on your dashboard, but it's rare that anyone's dashboard consists of all four of those common factors. Consider things such as:
- how many lives I touch,
- how many books I write,
- how many customers use my product,
- how much money I'm able to give, how many people I'm able to employ,
- how much love I give,
- how many days I walk in alignment with God,
- how many hugs I give,
- how many people I make smile,
- how many meals I share with others,
- how many hours I spend doing my passion.

These are all valid ways to measure success.

The worst feeling in the world is succeeding according to someone else's definition of success while you feel unsuccessful on the inside because their definition of success isn't the same as yours. Whether your parents and peers agree or understand how you measure success isn't the point—they just want to see you happy. At the end of the day, you have to live your life. Nobody can live it for you. Further, that which gets measured is what gets done.

## PERSONAL & CHARACTER SUCCESS STATEMENTS

**Directions:** Fill in the frequency, action verb, and measurement for the three personal success statements below.

**Example**:

By the end of ...*the year*............., I want to have *broken bread with* .........*365*...............
　　　　　　　　FREQUENCY　　　　　　　　　ACTION VERB　　　　　QUANTITY

..*different people and learned something new from each one of them*...................
　　　　　　　　　　　　AREA OF MEASUREMENT

1. By the end of *My college career*., I want to have ....*earned a*...... *3.5*...................
　　　　　　　　FREQUENCY　　　　　　　　　ACTION VERB　　　　QUANTITY

..*GPA*.............................................................................................................
　　　　　　　　　　AREA OF MEASUREMENT

2. By the end of ............................, I want to have ............................ ...........................
　　　　　　　FREQUENCY　　　　　　　　　ACTION VERB　　　QUANTITY

...........................................................................................................
　　　　　　　　　　AREA OF MEASUREMENT

3. By the end of ............................, I want to have .......................... ...........................
　　　　　　　FREQUENCY　　　　　　　　　ACTION VERB　　　QUANTITY

...........................................................................................................
　　　　　　　　　　AREA OF MEASUREMENT

**Related professions include:**.........................................................................

...........................................................................................................

...........................................................................................................

...........................................................................................................

## PROFESSIONAL & CAREER SUCCESS STATEMENTS

**Directions:** Fill in the frequency, action verb, and measurement for the three professional success statements below.

**Example:**

By the end of ....... *my life* ............, I want to have .... *inspired* ............ .... *1,000,000+* ......
                Frequency                                     Action Verb         Quantity

.. *people to D.R.E.A.M. awake and make a living doing what they love daily* ..........
                                     AREA OF MEASUREMENT

1. By the end of ... *Life* ..............., I want to have *successfully raised 3* .......
                    FREQUENCY                        ACTION VERB         QUANTITY

...... *children* .........................................................
                             AREA OF MEASUREMENT

2. By the end of .........................., I want to have ..................... .................
                    FREQUENCY                        ACTION VERB         QUANTITY

...........................................................................
                             AREA OF MEASUREMENT

3. By the end of .........................., I want to have ..................... .................
                    FREQUENCY                        ACTION VERB         QUANTITY

...........................................................................
                             AREA OF MEASUREMENT

**Related professions include:**.........................................................

...........................................................................

...........................................................................

...........................................................................

# 1.6 HOW TO IDENTIFY YOUR PASSIONS

We've all heard the expression: "Do what you love and the money will follow." However, this advice skips a step. Do you what you love, get great at what you do, and then the money will follow. It doesn't matter what your passion is, there is someone out there in the world making a living doing it. The question is not so much "How?" or "How much?" The real question is "How hard are you willing to work to crystallize your passion into a skill that others value?" If Joey Chestnut can win $10,000 for doing something as obscure as eating sixty-six hot dogs in twelve minutes at the Nathan's Hot Dog Eating Competition, then you can make a living doing whatever it is you love.

Let's begin by making a distinction between passions and interest because a lot of people use them synonymously when they aren't one and the same.

| INTERESTS | PASSIONS |
|---|---|
| Half-hearted Play | Disciplined Practice |
| Free Time (If I have time) | Full Time (I make time for it) |
| Topic-Based | Action-Oriented |

First and foremost, with an interest you aren't really focused on getting better. You just do it to play and have fun. With passions, you engage in disciplined practice because you are trying to get better and convert your love into a skill.

Secondly, when you're only interested in something, you let it slide if life gets busy. If you're passionate about something, it is integrated into your life just like sleeping, breathing, and eating. It's a priority that you won't compromise, no matter what else is going on any given day or week.

Finally, passions are action-based whereas interests are usually only topical. When you get specific about the action that you are passionate about, you can connect careers to that action (e.g., catching a baseball, hitting a baseball, collecting baseball cards, coaching baseball), but if you only know the general topic (e.g., baseball or sports), then it is harder to connect a career path to your interest. Being interested in something is a start, but in order to discover your passion you have to determine what action within that topic moves you.

Oftentimes, our passions are right around us because we naturally gravitate to them without even knowing it. If you don't know your passion, then the only way to discover it is by exposing yourself to new things. In this section, we're going to explore the things you already love doing to see if you can discover the passions that link them and, hopefully, find a common thread that reveals your true passion.

**PASSION FINDER**

*Play Sports*
*Making people laugh*

**Directions:** Complete the chart below with your favorite things in the first column and their associated passions in the second column. From there, consider careers that connect to that passion, no matter how random. The purpose of this exercise is to help you think creatively about your passions and how to apply them to your profession.

| MY FAVORITE BOOK IS... | THIS SPEAKS TO MY PASSION FOR... | RELATED CAREER PATHS INCLUDE... |
|---|---|---|
| The Alchemist<br><br>Catcher in the Rye | Seeking truth | Researcher |
| | Learning from life | Anthropologist |
| | Finding self | Monk |

~~Reading~~ Figuring things out on the fly    Drifter

| MY FAVORITE THING TO DO ALONE IS... | THIS SPEAKS TO MY PASSION FOR... | RELATED CAREER PATHS INCLUDE... |
|---|---|---|
| | | |
| | | |
| | | |

| MY FAVORITE THING TO DO WITH OTHERS IS... | THIS SPEAKS TO MY PASSION FOR... | RELATED CAREER PATHS INCLUDE... |
|---|---|---|
| | | |
| | | |
| | | |

| MY FAVORITE THING TO DO AT WORK IS... | THIS SPEAKS TO MY PASSION FOR... | RELATED CAREER PATHS INCLUDE... |
|---|---|---|
| | | |
| | | |
| | | |

| MY FAVORITE SUBJECT IN SCHOOL IS/ WAS... | THIS SPEAKS TO MY PASSION FOR... | RELATED CAREER PATHS INCLUDE... |
|---|---|---|
| | | |
| | | |
| | | |

| MY FAVORITE SUBJECT OUT OF SCHOOL IS... | THIS SPEAKS TO MY PASSION FOR... | RELATED CAREER PATHS INCLUDE... |
|---|---|---|
| | | |
| | | |
| | | |

| MY FAVORITE TV SHOW IS... | THIS SPEAKS TO MY PASSION FOR... | RELATED CAREER PATHS INCLUDE... |
|---|---|---|
| | | |
| | | |
| | | |

| MY FAVORITE BOOK IS... | THIS SPEAKS TO MY PASSION FOR... | RELATED CAREER PATHS INCLUDE... |
|---|---|---|
| | | |
| | | |
| | | |

| MY FAVORITE MOVIE IS... | THIS SPEAKS TO MY PASSION FOR... | RELATED CAREER PATHS INCLUDE... |
|---|---|---|
| | | |
| | | |
| | | |

| MY FAVORITE WEBSITE IS... | THIS SPEAKS TO MY PASSION FOR... | RELATED CAREER PATHS INCLUDE... |
|---|---|---|
| | | |
| | | |
| | | |

| MY FAVORITE SUPERHERO OR CARTOON CHARACTER IS... | THIS SPEAKS TO MY PASSION FOR... | RELATED CAREER PATHS INCLUDE... |
|---|---|---|
| | | |
| | | |
| | | |

| MY FAVORITE PRODUCT IS... | THIS SPEAKS TO MY PASSION FOR... | RELATED CAREER PATHS INCLUDE... |
|---|---|---|
| | | |
| | | |
| | | |

| MY FAVORITE COMPANY IS... | THIS SPEAKS TO MY PASSION FOR... | RELATED CAREER PATHS INCLUDE... |
|---|---|---|
| | | |
| | | |
| | | |

| MY FAVORITE NONPROFIT ORGANIZATION IS... | THIS SPEAKS TO MY PASSION FOR... | RELATED CAREER PATHS INCLUDE... |
|---|---|---|
| | | |
| | | |
| | | |

| MY FAVORITE VIDEO OR BOARD GAME... | THIS SPEAKS TO MY PASSION FOR... | RELATED CAREER PATHS INCLUDE... |
|---|---|---|
| | | |
| | | |
| | | |

| MY FAVORITE MUSICIAN IS... | THIS SPEAKS TO MY PASSION FOR... | RELATED CAREER PATHS INCLUDE... |
|---|---|---|
|  |  |  |
|  |  |  |
|  |  |  |

| MY FAVORITE SPORT IS... | THIS SPEAKS TO MY PASSION FOR... | RELATED CAREER PATHS INCLUDE... |
|---|---|---|
|  |  |  |
|  |  |  |
|  |  |  |

**The passions that came up most included:**.................................................................................

.................................................................................................................................................

.................................................................................................................................................

**The professional paths I want to explore more include:**...................................................

.................................................................................................................................................

.................................................................................................................................................

# HOW TO IDENTIFY A PROBLEM THAT MATTERS TO YOU

What have you seen, experienced, read, or heard that made you mad or sad? If you could snap your fingers and alleviate the world of one problem or pain, what would it be?

- Is it a personal problem that you've experienced, like a disease that you or someone close to you has had, bad customer service, lack of financial education, procrastination, or poor communication between people who supposedly love each other?

- Is it a social problem such as too much information on the Internet (solved by Google), lack of access to organic food (solved by Whole Foods), or inability to create and organize media that allows people to express themselves (solved by Apple)?

- Is it a question or problem that nobody before has solved, such as the Wright brothers asking themselves "Can humans fly?" or Henry Ford asking "Is there something better for transportation than the horse and carriage?" If so, can we make it affordable for the average American?"

Problems are important because every job or business opportunity is derived from a problem first. The vision of a problem-free world is inspirational, but even when one problem gets solved, its solution may create another problem. For example, we discovered how to use fossil fuels for our cars, but then the new problem of carbon emissions emerged. At the end of the day, a company that isn't solving a specific problem in the world will go bankrupt, and what's true for companies is true for its employees.

Albert Einstein once said: "No problem can be solved from the same level of consciousness that created it." This means that the problems challenge our creative limits and push us higher and higher on the totem pole of evolution. Many of the easy problems have already been solved by business and innovation, so the problems are only going to get more and more difficult, which also means greater and greater impact once solved.

The size of the problem you choose to solve will determine the size of your reward socially and, most of the time, financially. People who solve small problems earn small salaries. In this section, we want to discover the problem that moves you and that you would love to wake up and courageously face every day until you solved it because it's that important to you and others. From there, we can find industries, companies, or jobs that will allow you to get paid to solve that problem every day.

## PROBLEMS IN A BAD ECONOMY

Do problems increase or decrease when the economy is down? Problems increase when the economy is down. Therefore, if every job is connected to some sort of problem, then do job opportunities increase or decrease in a down economy? They increase. A down economy simply means that the problems people were solving with their current jobs aren't as valuable anymore. Therefore, the employee are taking more value from companies than they are creating.

When that occurs, companies lose profits and have to lay existing employees off. The only way to have an economic recovery is to hire new people who can solve more meaningful problems. So when a company is laying off employees, it doesn't mean they aren't hiring. In reality, they are creating space to sustain themselves and find new talent who can help them get back up.

## PROBLEMS IN A GOOD ECONOMY

Do problems increase or decrease when the economy is up? Problems increase again. The vision of a problem-free world is not real. Solutions to old problems only lead to new problems. For instance, the transportation solution that Henry Ford pioneered with the automobile is now causing high $CO_2$ emissions problems today. Einstein once said that "No problem can be solved from the same level of consciousness that created it," meaning that new problems lead us to higher levels of thinking. In a world with no problems, there are no jobs.

The type of problems that emerge in an up economy are different than those that emerge in a down economy. Abraham Maslow's Hierarchy of Needs can explain it best. From lowest to highest, our human needs are physiological, safety and security, love and belong, esteem and achievement, and self-actualization. In a down economy, the problems people face are around the lower needs. How will I pay rent? How will I feed my family? How can I avoid crime? When the economy is up, the problems that emerge shift toward the higher levels. How can I achieve my full potential? How can I find peace of mind? How can I experience more joy? But either way the economy goes, new problems are being created and the people in position to solve problems along the entire spectrum are most likely to succeed and endure economic cycles.

# MASLOW'S HIERARCHY OF NEEDS

## PERSONAL PROBLEM FINDER

**Directions:** Think of problems you see in your life and the lives of your family, friends, company, colleagues, customers, and community. Complete the following prompts for your personal and professional life to explore the problems that are currently present in your life and around you. Observe any patterns in the types of problems you see, and then choose three to focus on going forward.

**Personal Pain & Gain Points:**

Problems I have faced in my life:.................................................................................................

..........................................................................................................................................

Problems others close to me are facing:.......................................................................................

..........................................................................................................................................

**Social Problems:**

Social problems that make me mad/sad:......................................................................................

..........................................................................................................................................

Causes I've donated to or volunteered for:..................................................................................

..........................................................................................................................................

**Creative Questions:**

If I had one wish, I would put an end to the problem of:.................................................................

..........................................................................................................................................

Business ideas I've thought about but not acted on:.....................................................................

..........................................................................................................................................

**Related professions include:**..................................................................................................

..........................................................................................................................................

..........................................................................................................................................

..........................................................................................................................................

## PERSONAL PROBLEM FINDER

**Directions:** Based on your previous answers, list the three problems you could dedicate your life to solving and four related professional paths for each.

**Example:**

High Divorce Rates—Mediator, Match Maker, Family Counselor, Youth Psychologist

**Problem 1:**...................................................................................................................

**Related professions include:**

........................................................      ........................................................

........................................................      ........................................................

**Problem 2:**...................................................................................................................

**Related professions include:**

........................................................      ........................................................

........................................................      ........................................................

**Problem 3:**...................................................................................................................

**Related professions include:**

........................................................      ........................................................

........................................................      ........................................................

## PROFESSIONAL PROBLEM FINDER

**Directions:** If you have had an internship or any sort of work experience, think about problems you observed for the customer, in the product or service, and/or company culture and processes that you think could have been improved and list related professional paths.

**Customers' Needs:** The three biggest problems I hear our customers mention about their businesses are:

1...................................................................................................................................

2...................................................................................................................................

3...................................................................................................................................

**Related professions include:**...............................................................................

...................................................................................................................................

**Products & Services:** The three biggest problems I hear our customers mention about our products/services are:

1...................................................................................................................................

2...................................................................................................................................

3...................................................................................................................................

**Related professions include:**...............................................................................

...................................................................................................................................

**Company Culture & Processes:** The three biggest problems I hear my colleagues mention about our company are:

1...................................................................................................................................

2...................................................................................................................................

3...................................................................................................................................

**Related professions include:**...............................................................................

...................................................................................................................................

# 1.8 HOW TO IDENTIFY YOUR TARGET MARKET

Perhaps you don't know your passion or have a problem that you deeply care about, but maybe there is a group of people that you really care about that, you feel, are powerful, but underserved, marginalized, or unfulfilled. A lot of people immediately start thinking about poor people or hungry children, but everyone needs help in some sort of way regardless of their socioeconomic status.

In business, a **target market** is a group of people that has the most to gain from a particular product or service a company offers and is willing to pay at least enough to sustain the business. We want to explore who your target market is given whom you love, your strengths, and your skills.

A target market can be defined in many ways; for example:
• Age: millennials, baby boomers, children, the elderly
• Ethnicity: Asian, African-American, Hispanic, White
• Income: rich, poor, middle-class
• Spirituality: Christian, Muslim, Buddhist, Jewish, New Age, just spiritual
• Location: urban, rural, local, national, global
• Life Stage: teenagers, young adults, adults, retired, new parents, students
• Interests: yoga, service, bike riding, the arts, entrepreneurship, food, technology
• Shared Experiences: foster youth, alcoholism, cancer, women in leadership
• Shared Need: access to healthy food, good education, affordable housing, jobs

These are just some of the ways that you think about your target market. Your target market may be a combination of many of the above. Any business that isn't solving a problem for a person who is a part of a larger target market will not be in business for long. But if one person needs and values what you have to offer, then it is likely that there are many others who do as well.

By starting with your target market, you can ask and observe what their problems and needs are, and then zero in on the one that you are most passionate about solving. Your target market also helps you distinguish yourself from people who are generalists. It's easier to establish yourself in a niche than it is to establish that what you are offering to the world can serve everyone equally. In this section, you are going to create an imaginary customer and success story for someone you've served through your work so that you have a more vivid picture of the stories and impact you want to create. From there, you can explore career paths that will allow you to create that story daily for yourself and others. It's a natural human desire to want to help others, but the more specific you can get about how you like to help and whom you like to help, the more focused your career search will be.

## CUSTOMER TESTIMONY

**Directions:** Write a testimony from someone you want to serve. Address where that person is on their journey when you meet, how you served him/her, and where that person ended up as a result of your service. Create the character or pull from a true story.

My name is (Customer Name)...........................................and I was initially in a state of

.................................................................................................................................................

.................................................................................................................................................

.................................................................................................................................................

Before I met (Your Name)............................................, I was ❏ stuck and not going anywhere ❏ broken & not going fast enough ❏ lost & not going the right way. On my own, it was impossible for me to reach my desired state, which is

.................................................................................................................................................

.................................................................................................................................................

.................................................................................................................................................

(Your Name) ........................................ helped me get there by (What You Did)

.................................................................................................................................................

.................................................................................................................................................

.................................................................................................................................................

.................................................................................................................................................

As a result of his/her contribution, it is now possible for me to

...........................................................................................................................................

...........................................................................................................................................

This profound change in my life allows me to use my vehicle to positively

impact (Who They Serve)...............................................................................................

...........................................................................................................................................

**List 10 professional paths that would allow you to make this a true story:**

.................................................................     .................................................................

.................................................................     .................................................................

.................................................................     .................................................................

.................................................................     .................................................................

.................................................................     .................................................................

# 1.9  HOW TO FIND YOUR NICHE & POSITION YOURSELF TO WIN

Even given all of the amazing things you've done to get where you are today, most people have never committed to greatness at anything. We are comfortable with good enough. (I was good enough to graduate high school and get into this college. I was good enough to get into and complete my major. I was good enough to get an A- in that class.) The reason we settle for good enough is that up until this point, just being ahead of the curve was enough to get by. We have a tendency to want the greatest return for the least amount of effort.

However, even if you're the best at something in relationship to everyone else, that doesn't mean that you're at your personal best. Further, just because you're at your personal best doesn't mean that you will be the best in the world. Finding your niche means shrinking your playing field until you've mastered it and then expanding from there.

Let's use the career path of the late Michael Jackson, the most successful entertainer of all time. As a young boy, Michael Jackson committed to being the best lead singer for an R&B group, The Jackson Five. After mastering that, he became a great songwriter. From there he emerged as a solo artist. Then, without his brothers behind him, he committed to being one of the world's best dancers. As he mastered one part of music, another aspect emerged as his next challenge. Eventually, he became one of the world's greatest entertainers.

When you fully commit to the mastery of something, three things happen:

1. You master that specific skill or subject.
2. You master the process of mastery, which you can now apply to other things you want to master.
3. You master yourself, which is the highest form of mastery there is.

If someone said from the beginning, "Michael, you need to be the best singer, songwriter, dancer, and entertainer," he might have been overwhelmed, but since he was given time to mature as an artist, he was able to take on new things one at a time. The same goes with learning languages or instruments. If someone tells you to learn five languages or instruments at once, you won't make much progress, but if you are told to master a particular language or instrument first, you will find that after mastering one, mastering two, three, four, and five becomes much easier. Now it's time decide what you want to master first; unfortunately, it may not be related to your college major.

**SUPERHERO NAME EXAMPLES**

| PERSON | SUPER POWER | SUPERHERO NAME |
|---|---|---|
| Caesar Milan | The power to connect with dogs and train them to behave | Dog Whisperer |
| Troy Dunn | The power to help people locate long lost family members | The Locator |
| Jesus | The power to anoint people | Christ (Anointed One) |
| Muhammad Yunus | The power to create innovative financial models to empower entrepreneurs | Banker to the Poor |
| Oscar Pistorius | The power to run extremely fast with prosthetic legs | Blade Runner |
| Steve Irwin | The power to tame crocodiles and other animals | The Crocodile Hunter |
| Stephen Wiltshire | The power to capture complex images in his head (i.e., the entire birds-eye view of a city) and then draw it from memory despite having autism. | The Human Camera |

**More Names:** The Advocate, bReignStorm, CEO, Coach, The Connector, The Chancellor, Correspondence, The Creator, Dr. Grow, Dream Catcher, Elevator, The Enlightener, The Explorer, Exposure, The Gatekeeper, The Justice, The Innovator, The Life Guard, The Mayor, The Mirror, The Music Making Do-Gooder, The Negotiator, Nikki Numbers, Potential Pusher, The Prophet, Reflector, Sharp Shooter, Show Time, Storyteller, The Synthesizer, Truth Bearer, Truth Seeker, Poverty Killer, Voice of the Go Getter, The Warden, Well-Ness, Wellness Guru

**SUPERHERO NAMING**

**Directions:** Your name is a powerful form of branding, however your given name and job title likely don't communicate your value accurately. To identify a name that speaks to your brand, list all of the skills you have and subjects you know and then use that information to create a superhero name for yourself. Below are some examples of some modern day superheroes.

**What are your nicknames from childhood? sports? family? friends?**
*Example: My teammates called me The Visionary because of my court vision.*

................................................................................................................

................................................................................................................

**What are potential names based on your passions?**
*Example: The Connector for someone who is passionate about connecting people.*

................................................................................................................

................................................................................................................

**What are potential names, based on the problems you want to solve?**
*Example: The Healer for someone who wants to alleviate pain in the world.*

................................................................................................................

................................................................................................................

**My superhero name is:**................................................................................

**I'm committed to being the world's best at:**................................................

................................................................................................................

## SUPER SKILLS & SUBJECTS

**Directions:** Given your superhero name, list the skills and subjects that you want to perform well above average at or that people would expect you to perform well above average.

**MY SUPER SKILLS**

| SKILLS<br>I'm well above average at... | RELATED<br>PROFESSIONS |
|---|---|
|  |  |
|  |  |
|  |  |
|  |  |
|  |  |
|  |  |
|  |  |

**MY SUPER SUBJECTS**

| SUBJECTS<br>I'm well above average at... | RELATED<br>PROFESSIONS |
|---|---|
|  |  |
|  |  |
|  |  |
|  |  |
|  |  |
|  |  |
|  |  |

## SUPERPOWERS & PRACTICES

**Directions:** Now that you have a superhero name, list two super powers, skills, strengths, or abilities connected to your name and positioning. Come up with two **practice (a set of daily, weekly, or monthly actions to maintain progress)**. Your superhero should be consistent in your personal and professional life.

**Superhero Name:** The PurposeFinder

**Commitment:** To be the world's best at helping people find their purpose and make a living doing what they love.

**Example Power:** Ability to inspire people instantaneously

**Practice E.1:** Create conversations about life with two or more people weekly

**Practice E.2:** Read inspirational text for 30 minutes daily (3.5 hours/week)

**Power #1:**..................................................................................................................

My Practice 1:..............................................................................................................

My Practice 2:..............................................................................................................

I will do this ........ times/day or ........ times/week, which equals ........ hrs/week

**Power #2:**..................................................................................................................

My Practice 1:..............................................................................................................

My Practice 2:..............................................................................................................

I will do this ........ times/day or ........ times/week, which equals ........ hrs/week

**Related professions include:**.....................................................................................

...................................................................................................................................

...................................................................................................................................

# 1.10 HOW TO THINK LIKE A CAREER PIONEER

If you are lost and looking for direction, the best person to ask is someone who has been where you want to go. Wherever you're trying to go, there is likely someone who has already been there, and you can save yourself tons of time by finding, contacting, and asking those people the right questions. People who have been where you are trying to go professionally are considered **career pioneers**.

Who is where you want to be and doing what you want to do? This is a tough question to answer since you may not know exactly what you want to do or where you want to be. So in many ways, career discovery starts off like a game of pin-the-tail-on-the-donkey—at first you're way off, but over time you can feel when you're getting hotter or colder.

Your career pioneers don't have to be in the exact profession you want to be in. They should be people who love their work and deem themselves successful according to their own dashboard. A good question to start with is "Do you love what you do?" Unfortunately, that erases 80 percent of workers as an option, but you want to find someone in the 20 percent. Regardless of what they do for a living, you want to know how they got there, why they chose this profession, what they are passionate about, what they earn, and how they integrated work into their lifestyle.

This is called **career pathing**—the process of finding pioneers and mapping out how they got from where you are today to where they are today. If you career path the forty-four U.S. presidents, you will find that twenty-four out of forty-four were lawyers, and seventeen out of forty-four were congressmen or governors first. Becoming vice-president is the third most common way to becoming president, not the first. This is a huge insight, if you're considering running in the 2032 election.

## CAREER PATHING U.S. PRESIDENTS

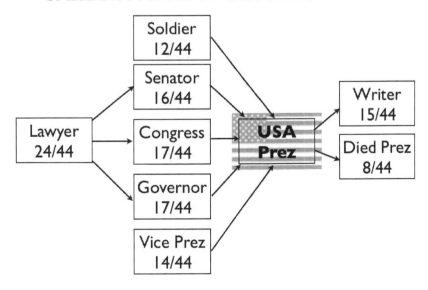

The two most important things you can do when researching a job are:
1. Figure out the path and patterns other people took to get a similar job, and
2. Find out where people who have had that job ended up.

It is likely that someone out there has done or is doing something similar to what you want to do, and you can learn valuable information from talking to him/her or reading his/her biography. Keep in mind that what worked for another person won't always work for you. Why? The world is changing extremely fast, and thus the game is changing. Whereas your pioneer may have worked at one company for a long time, your path to the top may involve multiple companies because of changes in the world economy.

In this section, you will identify two personal pioneers and two career pioneers. Then you will map out the career paths of your personal pioneers, using the provided list of interview questions and researching your career pioneers on the Internet.

## PIONEER INTERVIEWS

**Directions:** Interview at least one of your personal pioneers. Before asking your questions, tell that person why you chose to interview him/her and what you admire about him/her.

| PERSONAL PIONEER #1 | PERSONAL PIONEER #2 |
|---|---|
| Name: | Name: |
| Job Title: | Job Title: |

## CAREER QUESTIONNAIRE

- What did you think you were going to be when you grew up?
- How did that change and evolve over time?
- Do you love what you do now?
- In your eyes, what questions should I be asking myself as I navigate my career change?
- What tradeoffs have you had to make along the way regarding your time, family, and money?
- How much does it cost to maintain your current lifestyle?
- If you could do it all over again, what would you do differently (if anything)?
- I've discovered that I'm passionate about _____. Do you have any ideas about where I could apply this passion, or any connections to people you think I should talk to?

**NOTES:**

..............................................................................................................................

..............................................................................................................................

..............................................................................................................................

..............................................................................................................................

..............................................................................................................................

..............................................................................................................................

..............................................................................................................................

..............................................................................................................................

..............................................................................................................................

**CAREER PATHING**

**Directions:** Identify two of your path-specific professional pioneers and backtrack from where they are today to map out their career paths from college. Look for commonalities in the process.

| PROFESSIONAL PIONEER #1 | PROFESSIONAL PIONEER #2 |
|---|---|
| Name: | Name: |
| Job Title: | Job Title: |
| Background: | Background: |
| Education: | Education: |
| Companies: | Companies: |
| Functions: | Functions: |
| Other: | Other: |

# 1.11 HOW TO CREATE YOUR CAREER VISION

Traveling through life without a vision is like sailing a ship without a rudder—you end up adrift and your destination is controlled by the winds instead of your will. When you begin with the end in mind, you recognize the importance of a rudder because it helps you counter the winds when they are against you and use them to your advantage when they are for you.

Life is similar, except that the winds are defined by external factors that aren't in your control such as the state of the economy, Baby Boomers delaying retirement meaning fewer jobs for their children, and even things such as natural disasters. Despite these deterrents, you can still reach your desired destination if you control the controllables— the things within you that nobody else can determine such as your effort, discipline, and vision.

**Visioning** is the process of forecasting your future using your imagination, words, and images. You may have heard of vision boarding or collaging. They are processes by which people cut out words and images from magazines and other sources and paste them on a poster board to create a collective vision for their lives. The process is powerful because, as the individual flips through words and images, s/he has to say yes or no to each one. "Yes, this is what I want" or "Yes, this is who I truly am." In addition, even if you don't know what you want, the collage serves as a menu of options you can choose from to stimulate ideas and shape your vision.

Americans average ten jobs between the ages of eighteen and thirty-four, according to the U.S. Bureau of Labor Statistics in 2002, and that number has gone up to fourteen jobs in 2008. On top of that, only 2 percent of people surveyed claim to be working in the occupation they had planned when they were eighteen years old. Obviously, a lot of people are unclear about their career visions, but with forty years and a focused direction, you can get almost anywhere you want to go personally and professionally.

In this next section you will write a eulogy or eightieth birthday toast from the perspective of your best friend. It should capture your personal vision and character (who you want to be). For your professional vision, you will write a retirement speech after your forty-plus years of work to capture your career (what you want to be). Through these written exercises, you will begin to visualize where you ultimately want to end up, and your personal and professional visions will help you make decisions about which way to turn your rudder at turning points in your life.

**EULOGY OR TOAST**

**Directions:** Write a eulogy or a toast to yourself from the perspective of your best friend when you're eighty years old. Questions to consider include:

- What roles do I envision myself taking on throughout my life? (e.g., parent, community leader, entrepreneur).
- What do I hope to leave behind? (e.g., family business, lasting change, my art, legacy).
- What's one word, belief, or quote that people will remember me for? Why? (e.g., honest, authentic, inspirational).

............................................................................................................

............................................................................................................

............................................................................................................

............................................................................................................

............................................................................................................

............................................................................................................

............................................................................................................

............................................................................................................

............................................................................................................

............................................................................................................

............................................................................................................

............................................................................................................

............................................................................................................

............................................................................................................

............................................................................................................

**RETIREMENT SPEECH**

**Directions:** Imagine the last day of your career after forty years of hard work. Finally, retirement! Write a short speech outlining the value you created, the legacy you left, the lives you impacted, the growth you sparked and experienced, and the change you brought about in your organization(s), industry, and world.

...... years and ....... months from today, ................, ......., 20.......

.........................................................................................................................

.........................................................................................................................

.........................................................................................................................

.........................................................................................................................

.........................................................................................................................

.........................................................................................................................

.........................................................................................................................

.........................................................................................................................

.........................................................................................................................

.........................................................................................................................

.........................................................................................................................

.........................................................................................................................

.........................................................................................................................

.........................................................................................................................

.........................................................................................................................

.........................................................................................................................

.........................................................................................................................

# 1.12

## HOW TO LEAVE A LEGACY

Most people say they want to leave some sort of legacy in life. Even if they don't say it, there is usually some sort of desire. We all want to be remembered because being remembered means that our lives had meaning and significance to someone other than ourselves. The sad thing is most people don't leave a legacy; instead of leaving things that really *matter* and last forever, they leave behind *materials* that have short shelf lives.

Many spiritual teachers' such as Jesus, Confucius, Lao Tzu, and Buddha have left legacies that lasted millennia. Many inventors have left legacies that have lasted centuries like Alexander Graham Bell and the telephone or the Wright Brothers and the airplane. Artists like Leonardo DaVinci also leave legacies that last centuries. Some entrepreneurs and civic leaders leave legacies that last decades or centuries as well. Below are four ways that you can consider leaving a legacy through some sort of vehicle or body.

**1. Baby Bodies:** How great a parent are you committed to being?

This is perhaps the easiest way to leave a legacy because almost anyone can have a child. We know that if we have kids and then they have kids, then our name will live on. In essence, we're all a part of someone's legacy biologically, but simply having children limits your legacy to your family when your sphere of influence could actually be wider. The dilemma here is that some parents think they have to give up on their own legacy to ensure that their kids can leave a legacy, but we all have a legacy to leave whether we have kids or not.

**2. Body of Work:** What are you creating that could impact the world for decades or centuries?

Musicians, artists, filmmakers, actors, authors, athletes, inventors, and others leave legacies through bodies of work. They leave behind music, paintings, films, books, inventions, and more. The risk one takes to make a living doing what one loves—overcoming the predominant rumors of "the starving artist"—is great and not everyone makes it. However, those who push the envelope and challenge the assumptions, limitations, and status quo of their field, industry, or genre usually aren't forgotten because of their boldness and innovation. Examples include Michael Jackson, Charlie Chaplin, Edgar Allen Poe, George Washington Carver, Ben Franklin, and more.

**3. Institutional Body:** What spaces are you creating to empower other people?

Entrepreneurs, spiritual and civic leaders, and educational pioneers fit here. They create companies, nonprofits, governments, religions, colleges, universities, associations, and systems. The difference between a body of work and an institutional body is that an institutional body creates space for other people to grow and develop, whereas a body of work typically comes from an individual. The risk of creating an institutional body includes all of the risk associated with creating a body of work in addition to financing buildings, supporting other people, and pushing back from existing institutions that yours may threaten. Once they grow from their small cultish state to impacting overall culture, they become integrated into the fabric of society. However, unless institutions evolve beyond their founder's original vision and stay relevant to the times, they can become hollow buildings with no purpose except to keep going for the sake of existence.

**4. Body in Service:** What cause are you willing to die for?

Nuns, martyrs, soldiers, and servants to society give their bodies in service and they are remembered for their selfless sacrifice more so than something they created and left behind. The legacies of those assassinated—such as John F. Kennedy and Martin Luther King Jr.—will live on, not just because they were assassinated, but because of the beliefs and principles that they publicly stood for so strongly that caused their assassinations. Then there are servants to society such as soldiers and those, like Mother Theresa, who give up their lives and worldly possessions to ensure that the forgotten members of society are loved and supported.

In this next section, you will explore four ways you can leave your legacy. You will put dates on each commitment. For the fourth way, you will write another eulogy, but this eulogy should focus on who you were being throughout your life rather than what you were doing. You will also explore the questions:
• What is possible for people when you are present?
• How does your energy shift the energy of those around you?
• What do people feel when you enter the room?

No two legacies are the same—if they were the same, then they wouldn't be legacies. Your life has uniquely positioned you to be someone and do something that nobody else can due to a variety of factors—some in your control, others not—that have shaped who you are today. So what will your legacy be?

## 4 WAYS TO LEAVE YOUR LEGACY

**Directions:** Write the name/title of the bodies you intend to leave and the year you intend to create them below.

**1. Baby Bodies** (e.g., kids' names, foster youth, animals, guardian of..., etc)

............................................................................................Year ..................

............................................................................................Year ..................

............................................................................................Year ..................

............................................................................................Year ..................

............................................................................................Year ..................

**2. Bodies of Work** (e.g., writing, art, music, recipes, events, legislation, etc)

............................................................................................Year ..................

............................................................................................Year ..................

............................................................................................Year ..................

............................................................................................Year ..................

............................................................................................Year ..................

**3. Institutional Bodies** (e.g., for-profit, nonprofit, club, group, movement, etc)

............................................................................................Year ..................

............................................................................................Year ..................

............................................................................................Year ..................

............................................................................................Year ..................

............................................................................................Year ..................

## 4 WAYS TO LEAVE YOUR LEGACY

**Directions:** Write your eulogy, again from the perspective of your best friend, without mentioning anything from the other three bodies. This is more about who you were being versus what you were doing. Things to include are: the greatest lessons you learned from life, the principles you stood for and daily rituals, your relationship with your spiritual source, special thank-yous, favorite quotes, scriptures, sayings, your turning points, your greatest memories, your biggest fears and weaknesses, or your hopes and vision for the future.

### 4. Body in Service to Others

...............................................................................................................................

...............................................................................................................................

...............................................................................................................................

...............................................................................................................................

...............................................................................................................................

...............................................................................................................................

...............................................................................................................................

...............................................................................................................................

...............................................................................................................................

...............................................................................................................................

...............................................................................................................................

...............................................................................................................................

...............................................................................................................................

...............................................................................................................................

...............................................................................................................................

...............................................................................................................................

## PERSONAL IN-POSSIBILITY

**Directions:** Complete the following statements for your personal life based on the new possibilities you want to see for the different people you touch with your presence and actions.

**Because of my personal life….**

**my family will be able to…**

......................................................................................................................................

......................................................................................................................................

......................................................................................................................................

**my friends will be able to…**

......................................................................................................................................

......................................................................................................................................

......................................................................................................................................

**my community will be able to…**

......................................................................................................................................

......................................................................................................................................

......................................................................................................................................

**my world will be able to…**

......................................................................................................................................

......................................................................................................................................

......................................................................................................................................

## PROFESSIONAL IN-POSSIBILITY

**Directions:** Complete the following statements for your professional life based on the new possibilities you want to see for the different people you touch with your presence and actions.

**Because of my professional life....**

**my customers will be able to...**

..........................................................................................................................................

..........................................................................................................................................

..........................................................................................................................................

**my company will be able to...**

..........................................................................................................................................

..........................................................................................................................................

..........................................................................................................................................

**my colleagues will be able to...**

..........................................................................................................................................

..........................................................................................................................................

..........................................................................................................................................

**my industry will be able to...**

..........................................................................................................................................

..........................................................................................................................................

..........................................................................................................................................

# 1.13<sub>A</sub> HOW TO CREATE A 30 SECOND PITCH

A **30 second pitch** (or elevator pitch) is a powerful way to introduce yourself when meeting new people anywhere, especially at professional networking events. The 30 second pitch will help you connect with people on a deeper level after answering all of the basic rapport-building questions that begin conversations such as:
• What's your name?
• Where are you from?
• Where do you go to school?
• What are you majoring in?
• How about those Yankees?
• Great weather isn't it?

There are a variety of reasons you should have a 30 second pitch ready to go:
1. It can lead to a deeper conversation, relationship, or opportunities with those you share it with.
2. When it is clear and concise, it expands the number of people who understand what you do and the value you offer, thus increasing your social capital (who you know and who knows you.)

Your 30 second pitch should summarize:
• Who you are
• Why you are here
• What you do
• Why you do it
• How you do it
• The value you create for others.

The goal of your introduction is to communicate that you're valuable and available, not to get them to simply remember your name. Most people introduce themselves based on their past or present instead of their desired future. If you're trying to make a change and get somewhere you've never been before, it's best to introduce yourself based on where you're going as opposed to where you are today.

In this section, you are going to answer those questions using one of two 30 second pitch templates. Once you have something you like, you should get in front of the bathroom mirror or a webcam and rehearse until you can deliver it with confidence.

Although it's called a 30 second pitch, it's unlikely that you will ever just rattle it off in thirty seconds straight. After using it a few times, you will find that you can anticipate people's questions and weave your answers seamlessly into the conversation.

**30 SECOND PITCH**

**Directions:** Use the templates below to write a powerful 30 second pitch that you would feel comfortable delivering to someone in a professional setting such as a networking event or interview. Afterward, rehearse it until you can deliver it with confidence.

**Example:**

My name is ....... *Jullien Gordon* ............ and I'm a ..... *Purpose Finder* ...........................
　　　　　　　　YOUR NAME　　　　　　　　　　　　　YOUR POSITION OR SUPERHERO NAME

I'm interested in work that makes it possible for ...............................................................

........ *people who hate their jobs and want more out of life* ................................
　　　　　　　　　YOUR PEOPLE OR TARGET MARKET

to address........ *underemployment, unemployment, overwork, & underpay* ................
　　　　　　　　　　　YOUR PROBLEM OR PAIN/GAIN POINT

and experience/achieve....... *what it means to D.R.E.A.M. awake* ...........................
　　　　　　　　　　　　　　　YOUR POSSIBILITY

I have a .......... *Tony Robbins* ......................-like passion for.............................
　　　　　　　YOUR PIONEER

........ *helping people grow and create the life they always dreamed of* ...................
　　　　　　　　　　　YOUR PASSION

and I envision a world where... *everyone makes their highest contribution* ................
　　　　　　　　　　　　　　　YOUR PICTURE

**30 SECOND PITCH**

**Directions:** Use the templates below to write a powerful 30 second pitch that you would feel comfortable delivering to someone in a professional setting such as a networking event or interview. Afterward, rehearse it until you can deliver it with confidence.

My name is ............................................. and I'm a .........................................................
YOUR NAME                                    YOUR POSITION OR SUPERHERO NAME

I'm interested in work that makes it possible for ...............................................................

................................................................................................................................
YOUR PEOPLE OR TARGET MARKET

to address.........................................................................................................................
YOUR PROBLEM OR PAIN/GAIN POINT

and experience/achieve......................................................................................................
YOUR POSSIBILITY

I have a ...........................................................-like passion for.............................................
YOUR PIONEER

................................................................................................................................
YOUR PASSION

and I envision a world where.................................................................................................
YOUR PICTURE

**FREE FORM 30 SECOND PITCH**

My name is ................................................. and I'm a .....................................................
YOUR NAME                                   YOUR POSITION OR SUPERHERO NAME

...................................................................................................................................

...................................................................................................................................

...................................................................................................................................

...................................................................................................................................

...................................................................................................................................

...................................................................................................................................

...................................................................................................................................

...................................................................................................................................

...................................................................................................................................

...................................................................................................................................

...................................................................................................................................

...................................................................................................................................

...................................................................................................................................

...................................................................................................................................

...................................................................................................................................

...................................................................................................................................

...................................................................................................................................

...................................................................................................................................

# 1.13B HOW TO SHARPEN YOUR 30 SECOND PITCH DELIVERY

Before you even say a word, people have already made judgments about you based on how you're dressed, your posture, who you're with, how tall you are, your ethnicity, your gender, your hair, and your demeanor. You can change some of those things, but don't waste your time trying to please everyone because you can't.

The only moment you can really control is the present moment and how they perceive you when you finally get a chance to speak. When you do say a word, people will make judgments about you in the first 30 seconds of meeting you that can take 30 years to erase. It's up to you to make sure that those judgments are good ones versus bad ones or bland ones.

Your 30 second pitch is your opportunity to leave a lasting impression. In 30 seconds you can move someone from indifferent to intrigued, inspired, and engaged. It's rare that your 30 second pitch will ever just be a 30 second monologue. In most cases, it will play out in the form of a dialogue. In the course of that dialogue, there are a few messages you want to definitely communicate to the listener and they are:

**1. You matter:** Just by saying hello and acknowledging others' presence, you are showing them that they matter.

**2. I'm caring:** By affirming others you know, you show that you care about them and those around you.

**3. I'm independent:** Stating your superhero name rather than job title and company name shows you're an independent thinker even if you work for or with someone.

**4. I'm valuable:** Without bragging, articulate what you make possible for others.

**5. I'm available**: Show that you are open in case they want to hire or work with you.

**6. I'm listening:** By asking a sincere question you inherently convey you're listening.

**7. I'm a contribution to you:** Find a way to contribute to them in the moment.

**8. I'm giving:** You can give advice or information, or a connection or idea as a gift.

Using these eight underlying messages, practice your 30 second pitch in the midst of your everyday conversations until it flows fluidly and people are inspired by you.

**DELIVERY EXAMPLE**

| | |
|---|---|
| YOU MATTER<br>I'M CARING | **YOU:** Hi, how are you? My name is Jullien Gordon.<br><br>**OTHER:** I'm Michelle Smith.<br><br>**YOU:** Nice to meet you. Who or what brings you here this evening?<br><br>**OTHER:** I'm a good friend of Pip's. We used to work together at ACME Inc. And you?<br><br>**YOU:** My friend Bill Rutland invited me. He's over there. Great guy!<br><br>**OTHER:** So what do you do? |
| I'M INDEPENDENT | **YOU:** Well, I'm a PurposeFinder.<br><br>**OTHER:** A PurposeFinder. What's that? |
| I'M VALUABLE | **YOU:** I make it possible for people who hate their jobs and are dealing with underemployment, underperformance, and underpay experience what it means to make a living doing what you love.<br><br>**OTHER:** Interesting. I haven't heard of that one before. So you have your own company? |
| I'M AVAILABLE<br><br>I'M PASSIONATE | **YOU:** Actually, I'm not an entrepreneur. That's how I create value within companies. I'm really passionate about helping people and companies grow and create the life they always dreamed of and I envision a world where everyone is making their highest contribution. |
| I'M LISTENING | What are you passionate about?<br><br>**OTHER: [SHARES THEIR PASSION]** |

| | |
|---|---|
| **I'M A CONTRIBUTION TO YOU** | **YOU**: Interesting!<br><br>Have you met................................................ You two should really meet.<br><br>She's over there. I'll make sure to introduce you before the evening is over.<br><br>OR<br><br>I really need to put you in contact with my friend .................................. She shares your passion for .................................. and I think you two would have a great time together.<br><br>Have you read...............................................? It's a must read. It's a must read for someone with your interests.<br><br>Have you seen............................................ ? I think you would really enjoy it. |
| **I'M GIVING** | Have you heard of...............................................? You should check out their website because it's relevant to your work.<br><br>Let me write it down (on one of my business cards) for you. I'm also going to give you another one of my cards in case you meet anyone tonight or afterward that you think I should know. |

**NOTES:**

.................................................................................................................................

.................................................................................................................................

.................................................................................................................................

.................................................................................................................................

.................................................................................................................................

.................................................................................................................................

.................................................................................................................................

# 1.14   HOW TO EVALUATE WHAT ACTIVITIES FULFILL YOU

A job is more a series of tasks than a set of responsibilities. You can be responsible for a lot of stuff and not have to do anything. Perhaps that's the job most people want—a big title and a small to-do list. Since that isn't the case for most people, then the best job is going to be the one where you spend most of your time doing tasks that you enjoy.

It's tempting to take a job that sounds sexy to others. There are so many people working other people's dream jobs, but the person in the actual position doesn't like what they do. Instead of doing what sounds good, you have to do what feels good. If you have to make a tradeoff between sounding good for thirty seconds at an occasional networking event and feeling good doing what you love for 30 percent of your entire life, which would you choose?

The most common thing people in the career-discovery process say when asked "What do you like to do?" is "I like to help people." That's great, but it's too general. Great follow up questions include:
• Who are the people you like to help?
• How exactly do you like to help them?
• What problem do you like helping them overcome?

Your answers to these second-layer questions will give more insight into how you help most. Every job helps people in some way, in the same way that every company that is making money is helping people. If a company isn't helping people, it will go out of business.

## FINDING FLOW

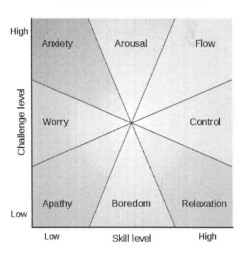

Ultimately, you want to find a job that allows you to achieve flow. **Flow** is the mental state in which a person in an activity is fully immersed in a feeling of energized focus, full involvement, and success in the process of the activity. When an athlete makes amazing plays in a consecutive stretch, that's being "in the zone" or "in flow," and you can experience that through work given the right skills and challenges.

In this section, we're going to explore your answers to the questions above as well as what your top five most fulfilling professional actions are. The list should include only things that you know you like doing because you've done them before and are still doing them today. Don't include things you think you like—try them first and then add them later. The best jobs are the ones where you can use what you love doing to help someone else solve a problem they have. Your D.R.E.A.M. job will be a forty-hour combination of these actions.

**FINDING FLOW**

**Directions:** Think about the things you love doing and all of the ways that you've helped people in the past. List 5 actions that you love doing that (could) help people in some way. For each action, specify who the action helped, what problem it helped them with, and then consider career paths that would allow you to help in that way full-time.

**Example:**

Action: *connecting people to other people, information, and ideas*
What does or could this action help? *people who feel like they are lost in life*
What problem does they action help others overcome? *missing out on great*
*opportunities that could possibly change their lives forever*
What careers would allow you help in this way? *marketing, community builder,*
*program coordinator, media, community website manager*

**Action #1:**.......................................................................................................

Who does or could this action help?.......................................................................

..............................................................................................................................

What problem does this action help them overcome?.............................................

..............................................................................................................................

What careers would allow you to help in this way?.................................................

..............................................................................................................................


**Action #2:**.......................................................................................................

Who does or could this action help?.......................................................................

..............................................................................................................................

What problem does this action help them overcome?.............................................

..............................................................................................................................

What careers would allow you to help in this way?.................................................

..............................................................................................................................

**Action #3**:........................................................................................................

Who does or could this action help?............................................................................

.....................................................................................................................................

What problem does this action help them overcome?.................................................

.....................................................................................................................................

What careers would allow you to help in this way?......................................................

.....................................................................................................................................


**Action #4**:........................................................................................................

Who does or could this action help?............................................................................

.....................................................................................................................................

What problem does this action help them overcome?.................................................

.....................................................................................................................................

What careers would allow you to help in this way?......................................................

.....................................................................................................................................


**Action #5**:........................................................................................................

Who does or could this action help?............................................................................

.....................................................................................................................................

What problem does this action help them overcome?.................................................

.....................................................................................................................................

What careers would allow you to help in this way?......................................................

.....................................................................................................................................

# 1.15  HOW TO ASSESS YOUR CURRENT SKILL SET

A **skill** is an action by which an individual can replicate success more frequently than the average person. Skills are one half of intellectual capital (what you know) and the other half is subject expertise. You can be skilled at navigating a task or a subject. However, just taking a class, or even getting certified, doesn't make one's knowledge of a subject a skill. A skill is something in which you can demonstrate proficiency or quality without question, AND move someone or something from some point A to some point B.

For example, a skilled accountant may be able to evaluate a company's financial health and balance its books with a certain level of accuracy faster than the average accountant. In addition, the skilled accountant has the ability to move a company from being financially oblivious (Point A) to financially aware (Point B). A skilled violin maker can take wood (Point A) and transform it into a beautiful instrument (Point B) that produces flawless sound.

There are many things that you know how to do well, but since the degree of difficulty isn't hard, you will not be able to create or capture much value in the market place for them. The more difficult it is for the average person to replicate your results, the more value you will be able to create and capture. For instance, millions of people are skilled at navigating Facebook, but since it is relatively easy to learn and do, it is hard to get paid to do it. On the other hand, there are people who actually code and program Facebook, which requires in-depth knowledge of various programming languages such as PHP and AJAX, which aren't as easy to learn or do. Therefore, they are able to create unique value and capture some of the value they create in the form of salary and, perhaps, stock options.

In this section, you will create a list of fifteen things you know how to do well. A great question to consider is: "If I had to teach a class on anything, what would it be?" Think of the unique things that you know how to do that have a degree of difficulty or require some expertise such as writing a business plan, speaking a foreign language, or leading a fifty-person student organization. Leave the easy stuff aside like tying your shoes or making a grilled cheese sandwich. After that, you will mark if you enjoy the activity. Some people get great at things they hate doing and get stuck doing what they hate for the rest of their lives. You want to avoid that and just get better at something you actually enjoy. From there you will identify a job, event, or story that proves you can do that skill well, and what exactly it is that you moved from a specific Point A to a specific Point B. Finally, you will name the skill and identify career paths that align with it.

**SOME SKILLS TO CONSIDER**

- administering programs
- planning agendas/meetings
- updating files
- advising people
- planning organizational needs
- setting up demonstrations
- analyzing data
- predicting futures
- sketching charts or diagrams
- assembling apparatus
- rehabilitating people
- writing reports
- auditing financial reports
- organizing tasks
- writing for publication
- budgeting expenses
- prioritizing work
- expressing feelings
- calculating numerical data
- creating new ideas
- checking for accuracy
- finding information
- meeting people
- classifying records
- handling complaints
- evaluating programs
- coaching individuals
- handling detail work
- editing work
- collecting money
- imagining new solutions
- tolerating interruptions
- compiling statistics
- interpreting languages
- confronting other people
- inventing new ideas
- dispensing information
- constructing buildings
- proposing ideas
- adapting new procedures
- coping with deadlines
- investigating problems
- negotiating/arbitrating conflicts promoting events
- locating missing information
- speaking to the public
- raising funds
- dramatizing ideas
- writing letters/papers/proposals questioning others
- estimating physical space
- reading volumes of material
- being thorough
- organizing files
- remembering information
- coordinating schedules/times managing people

- interviewing prospective employees running meetings
- selling products
- listening to others
- supervising employees
- teaching/instructing/training individuals
- relating to the public
- enduring long hours
- inspecting physical objects
- entertaining people
- displaying artistic ideas
- distributing products
- deciding uses of money
- managing an organization
- delegating responsibility
- measuring boundaries
- serving individuals
- mediating between people
- counseling/consulting people
- motivating others
- persuading others
- operating equipment
- reporting information
- summarizing information
- supporting others
- encouraging others
- delegating responsibilities
- determining a problem
- defining a problem
- comparing results
- screening telephone calls
- maintaining accurate records
- drafting reports
- collaborating ideas administering medication comprehending ideas
- overseeing operations motivating others
- generating accounts
- teaching/instructing/training individuals
- thinking in a logical manner making decisions
- becoming actively involved defining performance standards resolving conflicts
- analyzing problems recommending courses of action
- selling ideas
- preparing written communications
- expressing ideas orally to individuals or groups conducting interviews
- performing numeric analysis conducting meetings
- setting priorities

- setting work/committee goals developing plans for projects gathering information
- taking personal responsibility thinking of creative ideas providing discipline when necessary
- maintaining a high level of activity
- enforcing rules and regulations
- meeting new people
- developing a climate of enthusiasm, teamwork, and cooperation
- interacting with people at different levels
- picking out important information
- creating meaningful and challenging work
- taking independent action skillfully applying professional knowledge
- maintaining emotional control under stress
- knowledge of concepts and principles
- providing customers with service
- knowledge of community/ government affairs

## SKILLS INVENTORY

**Directions:** Create a list of fifteen things you know how to do well, and name the role, job, event, client, or story that demonstrates you know how to do that thing well.

| I KNOW HOW TO... (NOTE: DON'T USE "HELP" AS YOUR STARTER VERB. IT'S TOO VAGUE.) | LIST THE ROLE, JOB, EVENT, CLIENT, OR STORY YOU HAVE TO TELL ABOUT THIS SKILL |
|---|---|
| EX. *Get people motivated to move* | *Route 66 Tour* |
| 1 | |
| 2 | |
| 3 | |
| 4 | |
| 5 | |
| 6 | |
| 7 | |
| 8 | |
| 9 | |
| 10 | |
| 11 | |
| 12 | |
| 13 | |
| 14 | |
| 15 | |

## SKILLS INVENTORY

**Directions:** Identify the point A and point B of the person, place, or thing that you moved forward.

| POINT A:<br>WHERE AN INDIVIDUAL, ORGANIZATION, OR THING WAS BEFORE YOUR ACTION | POINT B:<br>WHERE AN INDIVIDUAL, ORGANIZATION, OR THING WAS AFTER YOUR ACTION |
|---|---|
| *unmotivated, depressed, stuck* | *motivated, alive, in motion* |
| 1 | |
| 2 | |
| 3 | |
| 4 | |
| 5 | |
| 6 | |
| 7 | |
| 8 | |
| 9 | |
| 10 | |
| 11 | |
| 12 | |
| 13 | |
| 14 | |
| 15 | |

## SKILLS INVENTORY

**Directions:** Mark if you enjoy doing the action. Determine what that skill would/could be called on a résumé. List the top two professional skills associated with the action.

| DO YOU LIKE THIS ACTION? | REVERSE SKILLS INVENTORY: WHAT WOULD YOU CALL THIS SKILL ON YOUR Résumé? | CAREER PATHS THAT REQUIRE THIS SKILL SET |
|---|---|---|
| X | *communicating with others* | *speaker, CEO* |
| 1 | | |
| 2 | | |
| 3 | | |
| 4 | | |
| 5 | | |
| 6 | | |
| 7 | | |
| 8 | | |
| 9 | | |
| 10 | | |
| 11 | | |
| 12 | | |
| 13 | | |
| 14 | | |
| 15 | | |

# 1.16 HOW TO IDENTIFY YOUR TOP 5 STRENGTHS

Whereas skills are actions that can help you get to where you want to be, **strengths** are characteristics that define who you already are. Strengths are internal and innate, and we each have a set. Like skills, you can learn how to use your strengths better, but skills improve through practice, whereas strengths improve through presence. Your strengths don't go away—they will always be with you. You just have to learn how to maximize them.

Unfortunately, we live in a world that teaches us to focus on our weaknesses instead of our strengths. If you come home with five As and one F, what do your teachers and parents have you focus on? The F. So while you're focusing on improving your weakness so that you can be a well-rounded kid, what do you think happens to the things you demonstrated strengths in? They deteriorate from lack of focus and presence. Ultimately you might pull up the F a little bit with a lot of effort, but at the end of the day, you end up average in everything. If you focused on your strengths instead, you could actually get better at using them and surpass what it means to have an A in a class and approach what it means to master something.

When you look at the world's most successful people, they aren't strong in everything, and they don't try to be. They identify where they are strong and put themselves only in situations that allow them to leverage their strengths. Where they have weakness, they find team members who are strong. Success isn't the result of mastering everything—success only requires the mastery of one or two subjects or skills. Furthermore, there are certain subjects and skills that you are uniquely positioned to master, given your strengths.

We highly recommend that you go to the bookstore and buy the book the Gallup *StrengthsFinder 2.0* and use the code inside to take the online test. The test will help you identify your top five strengths, and then the book will help you identify ways to integrate your strengths into every aspect of your life.

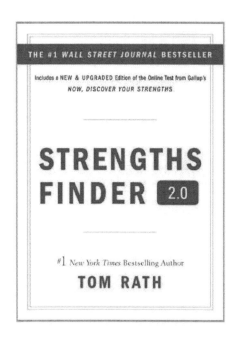

Once you have identified your strengths, you should look for stories from your past that demonstrate your use of each one. "What are your strengths?" is one of the top twelve interview questions, so you want to be able to answer it with conviction and context. But more importantly, knowing your strengths will prevent you from stepping into careers or companies that don't allow you to be at your strongest all of the time.

# EXERCISE 1.16

## GALLUP STRENGTHFINDER THEMES

**Achiever®** - People strong in the Achiever theme have a great deal of stamina and work hard. They take great satisfaction from being busy and productive.

**Activator®** - People strong in the Activator theme can make things happen by turning thoughts into action. They are often impatient.

**Adaptability®** - People strong in the Adaptability theme prefer to "go with the flow." They tend to be "now" people who take things as they come and discover the future one day at a time.

**Analytical®** - People strong in the Analytical theme search for reasons and causes. They have the ability to think about all the factors that might affect a situation.

**Arranger™** - People strong in the Arranger theme can organize, but they also have a flexibility that complements this ability. They like to figure out how all of the pieces and resources can be arranged for maximum productivity.

**Belief®** - People strong in the Belief theme have certain core values that are unchanging. Out of these values emerges a defined purpose for their life.

**Command®** - People strong in the Command theme have presence. They can take control of a situation and make decisions.

**Communication®** - People strong in the Communication theme generally find it easy to put their thoughts into words. They are good conversationalists and presenters.

**Competition®** - People strong in the Competition theme measure their progress against the performance of others. They strive to win first place and revel in contests.

**Connectedness®** - People strong in the Connectedness theme have faith in the links between all things. They believe there are few coincidences and that almost every event has a reason.

**Consistency® / Fairness™** - People strong in the Consistency theme (also called Fairness in the first StrengthsFinder assessment) are keenly aware of the need to treat people the same. They try to treat everyone in the world fairly by setting up clear rules and adhering to them.

**Context®** - People strong in the Context theme enjoy thinking about the past. They understand the present by researching its history.

**Deliberative®** - People strong in the Deliberative theme are best described by the serious care they take in making decisions or choices. They anticipate the obstacles.

**Developer®** - People strong in the Developer theme recognize and cultivate the potential in others. They spot the signs of each small improvement and derive satisfaction from these improvements.

**Discipline™** - People strong in the Discipline theme enjoy routine and structure. Their world is best described by the order they create.

**Empathy™** - People strong in the Empathy theme can sense the feelings of other people by imagining themselves in others' lives or others' situations.

**Focus™** - People strong in the Focus theme can take a direction, follow through, and make the corrections necessary to stay on track. They prioritize, then act.

**Futuristic®** - People strong in the Futuristic theme are inspired by the future and what could be. They inspire others with their visions of the future.

**Harmony®** - People strong in the Harmony theme look for consensus. They don't enjoy conflict; rather, they seek areas of agreement.

**Ideation®** - People strong in the Ideation theme are fascinated by ideas. They are able to find connections between seemingly disparate phenomena.

**Inclusiveness® / Includer®** - People strong in the Inclusiveness theme are accepting of others. They show awareness of those who feel left out, and make an effort to include them.

**Individualization®** - People strong in the Individualization theme are intrigued with the unique qualities of each person. They have a gift for figuring out how people who are different can work together productively.

**Input®** - People strong in the Input theme have a craving to know more. Often they like to collect and archive all kinds of information.

**Intellection®** - People strong in the Intellection theme are characterized by their intellectual activity. They are introspective and appreciate intellectual discussions.

**Learner®** - People strong in the Learner theme have a great desire to learn and want to continuously improve. In particular, the process of learning, rather than the outcome, excites them.

**Maximizer®** - People strong in the Maximizer theme focus on strengths as a way to stimulate personal and group excellence. They seek to transform something strong into something superb.

**Positivity®** - People strong in the Positivity theme have an enthusiasm that is contagious. They are upbeat and can get others excited about what they are going to do.

**Relator®** - People who are strong in the Relator theme enjoy close relationships with others. They find deep satisfaction in working hard with friends to achieve a goal.

**Responsibility®** - People strong in the Responsibility theme take psychological ownership of what they say they will do. They are committed to stable values such as honesty and loyalty.

**Restorative®** - People strong in the Restorative theme are adept at dealing with problems. They are good at figuring out what is wrong and resolving it.

**Self-Assurance®** - People strong in the Self-assurance theme feel confident in their ability to manage their own lives. They possess an inner compass that gives them confidence that their decisions are right.

**Significance®** - People strong in the Significance theme want to be very important in the eyes of others. They are independent and want to be recognized.

**Strategic™** - People strong in the Strategic theme create alternative ways to proceed. Faced with any given scenario, they can quickly spot the relevant patterns and issues.

**Woo®** - People strong in the Woo theme love the challenge of meeting new people and winning them over. They derive satisfaction from breaking the ice and making a connection with another person.

**STRENGTHS FINDER**

**Directions:** Get your top five strengths from the *StrengthsFinder 2.0* online test results or by choosing from the list and write an example that demonstrates the strength.

**Strength #1:**.............................................................................................................

Example:.....................................................................................................................

....................................................................................................................................

....................................................................................................................................

**Strength #2**...............................................................................................................

Example:.....................................................................................................................

....................................................................................................................................

....................................................................................................................................

**Strength #3:**.............................................................................................................

Example:.....................................................................................................................

....................................................................................................................................

....................................................................................................................................

**Strength #4:**.............................................................................................................

Example:.....................................................................................................................

....................................................................................................................................

....................................................................................................................................

**Strength #5:**.............................................................................................................

Example:.....................................................................................................................

....................................................................................................................................

....................................................................................................................................

**STRENGTH TO WEAKNESS**

**Directions:** Prepare for the "What's your greatest weakness?" question by considering the potential negative consequences when one of your strengths is overused.

1. Choose one of your five strengths:.................................................................................

2. Name that strength when it is overused:......................................................................
(e.g. When the strength "initiator" is overused, it comes off as "impatient.")

3. Write an example of how you overused a strength, and it became a weakness for that moment:

................................................................................................................................

................................................................................................................................

................................................................................................................................

................................................................................................................................

................................................................................................................................

................................................................................................................................

................................................................................................................................

................................................................................................................................

................................................................................................................................

................................................................................................................................

................................................................................................................................

................................................................................................................................

................................................................................................................................

................................................................................................................................

................................................................................................................................

................................................................................................................................

1.  CREATE YOUR
    D.R.E.A.M. LIFE

2.  **ATTRACT YOUR
    D.R.E.A.M. CAREER**

3.  BUILD YOUR
    D.R.E.A.M. TEAM

4.  LAND YOUR
    D.R.E.A.M. JOB

# 2.1  HOW TO DISCOVER GREAT CAREERS YOU NEVER CONSIDERED

In a survey of 3,891 United States teenagers, Bidwell, Csikszentmihalyi, Hedges, and Schneider discovered that 55 percent of teenagers expected to have one of only ten jobs when they grew up. That's very limiting considering that the number of career paths that exist is practically limitless. Among these students, 17 percent expect to be doctors or lawyers, but doctors and lawyers make up less than 1 percent of the American workforce. Additionally, 6 percent of teenagers expect to become professional athletes, yet professional athletes make up less than 0.1 percent of the American workforce.

| Occupation | Rank | % of sample |
|---|---|---|
| Doctor | 1 | 10 |
| Business Person | 2 | 7 |
| Lawyer | 3 | 7 |
| Teacher | 4 | 7 |
| Athlete | 5 | 6 |
| Engineer | 6 | 5 |
| Nurse | 7 | 4 |
| Accountant, CPA | 8 | 3 |
| Psychologist | 9 | 3 |
| Architect | 10 | 3 |
| Other | - | 45 |

So what influences your career choices? Parents, peers, television, other adults, on-campus recruiting, your school, your major, the economy, and the region you're in are all huge factors in your career exposure. However, sometimes, all of these things can limit your career exposure as well if you are more concerned about pleasing others than doing what pleases you.

Similar to dining out at a new restaurant, in order to make an informed career choice, it's best to take an in-depth look at the full menu, not just the top ten dishes. Now is the time to try out new things to find out what you really like before committing to an uninformed choice. It's frustrating when you order something safe, and then everyone else who took a risk ends up with a better tasting dish than you.

In this section, we want to help you get to your authentic career choice rather than the career choices that have been influenced by others. Therefore, you will do a few exercises that will help you understand why you want to be what you think you want to be, and open you up to new career possibilities. When it comes to career paths where you feel uncertain, ask someone who has been where you want to go.

## A-Z CAREER PATHS

**Directions:** Set a timer for four minutes. Write down a potential career path starting with each letter of the alphabet (e.g., A = architect, B = banker). Be as original and innovative as possible.

| | | | |
|---|---|---|---|
| A | | N | |
| B | | O | |
| C | | P | |
| D | | Q | |
| E | | R | |
| F | | S | |
| G | | T | |
| H | | U | |
| I | | V | |
| J | | W | |
| K | | X | |
| L | | Y | |
| M | | Z | |

**How long did it take you?** _____:_____
  MIN       SEC

**Find lots of answers at: http://www.bls.gov/oes/current/oes_stru.htm**

## PASSIONS + STRENGTHS + SKILLS

**Directions:** List your top passions, strengths, and skills in the associated boxes below. In the middle space, list career paths that come to mind that would allow you to do what you love and are great at what you love while leveraging your strengths.

2. TOP STRENGTHS

........................................

........................................

........................................

........................................

1. TOP PASSIONS

........................................

........................................

........................................

........................................

........................................

........................................

4. TOP CAREER PATHS

........................................

........................................

........................................

........................................

3. TOP SKILLS

........................................

........................................

........................................

........................................

## #1 CAREER EXPECTATIONS

**Directions:** Determine your #1 career choice. Answer the questions below to determine how certain you are that your desired career will get you what you want.

#1 Career Choice:.................................................................................................................

Where and when did I first learn or hear about this career path?

.............................................................................................................................................

.............................................................................................................................................

What are the top 3 reasons I want to work in this field?

1. ........................................................................................................................................

2. ........................................................................................................................................

3. ........................................................................................................................................

Who would think this career path is awesome?

❏ Me  ❏ My parents  ❏ My friends  ❏ A potential life partner  ❏ Anyone

| | YES | NO |
|---|---|---|
| Am I 100% certain this career path will give me what I want? | | |
| Have I interned or shadowed someone in this career? | | |
| Have I talked to someone in depth about it about this career? | | |
| Am I extremely passionate about what I will do day-to-day? | | |
| Am I willing to commit my entire career to this exact work? | | |
| Do I have all of the information I need to make a choice? | | |

Before I commit, what other questions should I ask or what else should I do?

.............................................................................................................................................

.............................................................................................................................................

How do I know this is what I really want?

.............................................................................................................................................

.............................................................................................................................................

## #2 CAREER EXPECTATIONS

**Directions:** Determine your #2 career choice. Answer the questions below to determine how certain you are that your desired career will get you what you want.

#2 Career Choice:..................................................................................................

Where and when did I first learn or hear about this career path?

..................................................................................................................................

..................................................................................................................................

What are the top 3 reasons I want to work in this field?

1. ...........................................................................................................................
2. ...........................................................................................................................
3. ...........................................................................................................................

Who would think this career path is awesome?

❒ Me    ❒ My parents    ❒ My friends    ❒ A potential life partner    ❒ Anyone

| | YES | NO |
|---|---|---|
| Am I 100% certain this career path will give me what I want? | | |
| Have I interned or shadowed someone in this career? | | |
| Have I talked to someone in depth about it about this career? | | |
| Am I extremely passionate about what I will do day-to-day? | | |
| Am I willing to commit my entire career to this exact work? | | |
| Do I have all of the information I need to make a choice? | | |

Before I commit, what other questions should I ask or what else should I do?

..................................................................................................................................

..................................................................................................................................

How do I know this is what I really want?

..................................................................................................................................

..................................................................................................................................

# 2.2

## HOW TO RESEARCH CAREERS OFFLINE & ONLINE

Learning becomes knowing, so the only way to know if a career is right for you is to learn about it in the most in-depth way possible. Finding a career that fits you doesn't have to be like a blind date. There are tons of resources and things you can do to get more information about a particular career path before your first interview.

As you can see from the diagram the highest form of learning is to participate in the activity. From a career perspective, that means doing the actual work as an intern, part-timer, or full-time employee. Other ways to engage in the work at a high level include job shadowing (via an on-campus club that engages in the work) or starting a company for the time being that does similar work on a smaller scale.

In fact, one of the keys to getting ahead in the interview process is to show that you've essentially been doing the work of an entry level employee already through personal projects, your own business, free work for your student group and friends, or internships. Let's say that you want to be an accountant. You can serve as your student group treasurer, do other people's taxes, or work part-time in the school's financial aid office or the financial department of the student store. These experiences will set you apart from someone who only majors in accounting.

When you have experience with the work under your belt before the interview, even if the experience isn't exactly the same, it shows that you really know what you want and have taken the time to test the waters before jumping in.

## HOW DO WE LEARN?

ACTION LEARNING

VISUAL LEARNING

VERBAL LEARNING

Participate In Activity
100%

Simulate The Activity
90%

Teach The Activity
70%

Watch Demonstration
50%

Watch Moving Pictures
40%

View Pictures
30%

Hear Words
20%

Read
10%

HOW MUCH DO WE REMEMBER?

## ONLINE RESOURCES

**Directions:** Choose one of your target companies. Visit the following website to see what information they have about it.

**Company Websites:** Find out about the mission, opportunities, what makes them unique, office location, etc.

.................................................................................................................................

.................................................................................................................................

.................................................................................................................................

**Vault.com**: Find industry rankings and news, company ranking, professional paths, and tips.

.................................................................................................................................

.................................................................................................................................

**Salary.com:** Find salary and salary trajectory for certain positions.

.................................................................................................................................

.................................................................................................................................

**LinkedIn.com:** Find friends who work at your target companies. Find industry related groups. Find news about companies (e.g., new hires, alumni from your school, etc.).

.................................................................................................................................

.................................................................................................................................

**GlassDoor.com:** Find employee testimonials and ratings for companies.

.................................................................................................................................

.................................................................................................................................

**Google News:** Find the latest news and trends when you type in companies or industries that interest you.

.................................................................................................................................

.................................................................................................................................

## OFFLINE RESOURCES

**Directions:** Choose one of your target companies. Do the following activities to see what information you can find about it.

**Annual Reports:** Find out about the company's financial performance as well as its the strategic direction and changes.

.................................................................................................................................

.................................................................................................................................

.................................................................................................................................

**Networking:** Find out in real time about companies and the jobs people have.

.................................................................................................................................

.................................................................................................................................

.................................................................................................................................

**Informational Interviews:** Find out why an individual chose one company over another. Find out what that person likes and doesn't like about the job. Find out about any upcoming new strategic initiatives.

.................................................................................................................................

.................................................................................................................................

.................................................................................................................................

.................................................................................................................................

**Job Shadowing:** Find out about company culture through observation. Find out if you like this kind of work.

.................................................................................................................................

.................................................................................................................................

**Internship (Paid or Unpaid):** Find out if you can see yourself doing this every day.

.................................................................................................................................

.................................................................................................................................

# 2.3 HOW TO EVALUATE THE ECONOMIC ENVIRONMENT

The world that your parents' generation graduated into is a lot different from the world you are graduating into. When your parents' generation graduated from high school, they only had to compete against the person sitting to their left or their right, and if they outperformed that person, they would be okay. However, for your generation, the competition has increased. Your parents had to outperform everyone in the country in order to get into the best private universities and everyone in their state to get into the best public universities. Now, because of globalization and the expansion of the Internet, you are competing against everyone in your age group in the entire world. So if you expect to do what your parents did, or even your older sibling(s), and get the same results, it's unlikely to occur. You have to work harder and do something different.

Since college is supposed to be preparing you for the real world, we need to know what the real world expects of college graduates. If your current educational experience isn't preparing you for what the real world require in terms of skills and strengths, then you have to commit to developing those things on your own. Oftentimes college students get caught in a four-year bubble. For many, college is the closest thing to utopia there is. But if you wait until reality strikes at graduation and that bubble bursts, you are starting off at a serious disadvantage.

In this next section, you will do a S.W.O.T. Analysis. **S.W.O.T.** stands for Strengths, Weaknesses, Threats, and Opportunities. Your strengths and weaknesses are internal, and they include everything you have such as your **four capitals** (personal, intellectual, social, and financial), and everything you don't have that you think you need to get what and where you want. Your threats and opportunities are external, and they include factors that you can't control (e.g., economic downturn) that work for or against you. Opportunities come from asking yourself "Given the current reality, in what ways am I well positioned to succeed?"

Completing your S.W.O.T. analysis involves doing some soul searching and some external research about trends in the world, the economy, and your target industry. In addition, you need to look at current events that may have positive or negative long-term impacts on your career. Understanding the lay of the land will help you navigate it better so that you can achieve your career aspirations.

## S.W.O.T. ANALYSIS QUESTIONS TO CONSIDER

| STRENGTHS & WEAKNESSES | OPPORTUNITIES & THREATS |
|---|---|
| **Personal Capital**<br>- What are your personal strengths?<br>- What are your professional strengths?<br>- What are your passions?<br><br>**Intellectual Capital**<br>- What skills or subjects do you claim to be an expert at?<br>- What certificates, licenses, degrees, or trainings have you completed?<br>- What other languages do you know? Spanish? French? HTML? PHP?<br><br>**Social Capital**<br>- Name 10 older people who can help you.<br>- Who are your professional mentors?<br>- What local and national professional organizations are you connected with?<br><br>**Financial Capital**<br>- How much financial freedom do you have?<br>- Do you have other sources of income besides your paycheck?<br>- How liquid are your assets? | **Personal**<br>- What is your personal risk tolerance?<br>- How many dependents do you have?<br>- How is your physical, mental, and emotional health?<br>- What have you been studying, reading, and learning to stay ahead of the curve?<br><br>**Industry**<br>- What trends do you see in your industry that are working for or against you?<br>- Is your industry growing or fading? Would you invest money in it today?<br>- What new innovations are on the horizon that can destroy or resurrect your industry?<br>- How many people do you know at companies that interest you? How much influence do they have?<br>- What have your created or done that has been extremely valuable in the past 3 years?<br><br>**Local, National, & Global**<br>- What trends do you see locally, nationally, or globally that are working for or against you? |

**S.W.O.T. ANALYSIS**

**Directions:** Consider your personal, intellectual, social, and financial capital and, in the left column, write where you have strengths (e.g., strong communicator, $20,000 saved up, diverse network in finance, etc.) and, in the right column, write down how you would like to grow in a given area (e.g., no connections in the industry, know only one language, $80K in debt, job hopping since college, etc.).

| STRENGTHS | WEAKNESSES |
|---|---|
| Personal Capital I have: | Personal Capital I need to develop: |
| Intellectual Capital I have: | Intellectual Capital I need to develop: |
| Social Capital I have: | Social Capital I need to develop: |
| Financial Capital I have: | Financial Capital I need to develop: |

## S.W.O.T. ANALYSIS

**Directions:** Given your strengths and capital, write in the box in the left column what opportunities are on your horizon based on your strengths in box one in the left column (e.g., start a marketing company with Billy, move to California's booming Silicon Valley, join Acme's product development team, go back and get my JD/MBA). Given your weaknesses and lack of capital, write in the right column what threats are on your horizon based on your weaknesses in the right column(e.g., industry shifting toward automation, jobs being outsourced, my skills are becoming less relevant every day).

| OPPORTUNITIES | THREATS |
|---|---|
| Personal: | Personal: |
| Professional: | Professional: |
| National & Global: | National & Global: |

# 2.4 HOW TO GET YOUR FRIENDS' INSIGHTS ON YOUR PERSONAL BRAND

Sometimes those close to us can articulate who we are better than we can. Our friends, family, and colleagues can see things in us that we can't see in ourselves because we think that the things that come naturally to us also come naturally to others, but they don't. Our value to others may be different than what we think, and we attract people based on our value to them.

So the best people to ask about your personal brand are those who have chosen to create relationships with you. Who knows you best? Who has observed you for a long time? Who just met you and what is their impression of you? In the business world, the process of asking for feedback about the qualities of who you are being and the quality of what you are doing is called **360-degree feedback**.

A clear distinction needs to be made between doing and being. Most people define who they are by what they do when, in fact, who you are should define what you do. Doing relates to outward manifestations of who you are. It's what emerges after decades of work. It includes your achievements, outer success, and personal gains in the eyes of the public. Your being is more internal. It has to do with who you are on a daily basis. It's more about your character than your specific career. It's about who you are, how you feel on the

| DOING | BEING |
|---|---|
| Outward | Inward |
| Decades | Daily |
| Creations | Character |
| Achievements | Achille's Heel |
| Outer Success | Inner Emotions |
| Gain | Gratitude |
| Public | Private |

inside, and your gratitude and appreciation for the gifts given to you that you are able to give to the world. Hopefully, your character and career align.

Those who know you best will be able to speak to both parts of you. Not only do they love being around you when you're doing nothing, but they also love to see what you do and who you are as you do it. What you achieve says a lot about who you are, but your personal brand goes into more depth about the back story that explains why you do what you do and why you were essentially born to do this career in this way.

What others say about you is more credible than what you say about yourself. It's not who you know, it's how well others know you, and in what context. Your insights from friends can be used for letters of recommendation, LinkedIn recommendations, interview answers, your 30 second pitch, or your biography.

**THE SUPERHERO SURVEY**

**Directions:** Superheroes know their superpowers. Do you? Sometimes our powers come so naturally to us that we don't even recognize them ourselves. So here's a fun survey to send to friends to get some 360-degree feedback and discover your superpowers. Then, you can figure out how they can be used professionally.

Warning: Side effects include increased happiness, greater self-awareness, and stronger friendships.

**STEP 1. Cut, copy, paste, & edit the e-mail template below.**

Subject: Who do you think I could be?

Hey,

I hope all is well.

As you know, I'm always looking to grow and I value what you think about me. I found this fun survey for friends to give feedback to one another regarding their strengths, passions, and careers. I'm sending it to only five people and one of them is you!

Can you please take five minutes to complete the survey at the link below? It's only six quick questions. Your answers will help me tremendously as I consider what's next for me. The more specific your answers, the better.

http://www.innerviewing.me/superhero-survey

I'll share with you what I discover about myself.

Sincerely,

**STEP 2. Select five close friends to whom you will send this e-mail.**

Above are examples of the types of people you may want to send the e-mail to. Make sure you choose five or more people you think will be honest with you and have demonstrated commitment to your success in the past.

They will take the survey and you will get this...

| | |
|---|---|
| Your Name * | ▉▉▉▉▉▉▉▉▉▉▉▉▉▉▉ |
| Your Email * | ▉▉▉▉▉▉▉▉▉▉▉▉▉▉▉ |
| Name of the friend who sent this to you: * | ▉▉▉▉▉▉▉▉▉▉▉▉▉▉▉ |
| The email address that they sent it from: * | ▉▉▉▉▉▉▉▉▉▉▉▉▉▉▉ |
| 1. POWERS: If you had to give your friend a nickname or superhero name, what would it be? And why? | La Paciente (The Patient One)-this is the first thing that came to mind. She shows great discipline and sticks through things even when they are hard. |
| 2. PASSIONS: What activities would you say your friend is most passionate about doing? And why? | She is passionate about healthy living. I'm always impressed with your ability to stick to exercise routines and healthy eating. Great w/ budgets and coordination. You are also passionate about fashion and you are very stylish. You have a good eye for putting things together. |
| 3. POTENTIAL PATHS: What potential professional paths could you see your friend being great at? And why? | Nutritionist, Stylist, Fashion Consultant, Own a business, Museum work, Women's Wellness |
| 4. PERFORMANCE: When have you see your friend exhibit excellence? What impressed you about it? | I'm impressed by her ability to manage her lifestyle. she travels, manages her time well and is very independent. she can make decisions and move on. she's thoughtful and not impulsive which provides here with security. |
| 5. RECOMMENDATIONS: Are there any companies, organizations, books, websites, or people you recommend they explore based on your suggestions above? | Def. the Alchemist<br>Start Where You Are: A Guide to Compassionate Living by Pema<br>Salvation: Black People and Love and All About Love by Bell Hooks<br>Start Tapping the Power Within by Iyanla Vanzant<br>Finding Soul on the Path of Orisa by Tobe Melora Correal<br>Books by Thich Nhat Hanh<br>TED videos r great.<br>I can help identify people once I know which direction you're heading. |
| 6. PEER SUPPORT: How do you hope to continue supporting your friend on the journey of life? | I don't have money but I can listen, share ideas, connect w/ people and u can come visit me. :) |
| 6a. What resources are you willing to contribute specifically: | • My time<br>• My network<br>• LOVE<br>• Advice/Ideas |

# 2.5 HOW TO GET GREAT RECOMMENDATIONS

Letters of recommendations are powerful statements of your credibility. Résumés are biased because they are written by you and are probably embellished a little bit to make you sound perfect. But when someone else's observations support things you mentioned in your résumé, it makes you a more believable candidate and a less risky hire.

Your letter of recommendation should come from people with credibility themselves. Their credibility will be derived from their names, positions, and years of experience. It's great to get recommendations from professors, former managers, community leaders (e.g., your church or an organization you volunteered for), coaches, and mentors. When you get a recommendation from a former manager, it conveys that you didn't leave on bad terms, and that you actually created value in a past workplace. The more recent the recommendation, the better. In fact, you should try to get recommendations anytime you're considering making a transition so that you have a track record of success to show. You are trying to convince a potential employer that you are guilty of being a perfect fit for the job and your recommendation writers are your eye witnesses.

When requesting a recommendation, you should make sure to provide your résumé, the job description, and three bullet-points you want the writer to address in the letter based on experiences you had together. The letter should follow this outline and address these questions and criteria:
• Who is the person making the recommendation? Why is this person credible?
• How does this person know you? How well does he or she know you?
• What has this person observed about your work, in general?
• Provide three supporting examples.
• Conclude with a recommendation to hire you.

In some cases, you may have to write the first draft of the recommendation yourself. This gives you the freedom to highlight experiences that you had with the recommender that he or she may not remember but are extremely relevant to the new position you're applying for.

In the end, strong letters of recommendation make the claims you've made in your cover letter and résumé more concrete and believable. Anytime you can take risk or uncertainty out of the hiring process for the potential employer, the easier you make it for them to hire you.

## LETTERS OF RECOMMENDATION

**Directions:** Identify three senior professionals who know who you are and can vouch for the quality of your work. See if they have a LinkedIn.com profile. Send the e-mail template below to them. If you don't get a response via e-mail, follow up with a call. If necessary, offer to write the testimonials for them first. Send thank you cards immediately after receiving the testimonials.

| NAME | WHAT QUALITIES CAN THEY SPEAK TO ABOUT YOU? |
|------|---------------------------------------------|
| Sean Morris | My project management and team leadership skills |
|  |  |
|  |  |
|  |  |

## E-MAIL TEMPLATE

Hi Mike,

I hope all is well with you and your family.

**Purpose:** I'm writing to:
1. Ask you if it's okay to put you down as a reference on my résumé.
2. Get a 3-5 sentence testimonial from you that speaks to who I am and the quality of my work.

**Context:** I've been doing some deep introspection lately and I'm positioning myself for my next career move.

**Usage:** I will include your testimonial in the references section of my résumé along with two others. If you have a LinkedIn account, it would help a lot if you recommended me there as well by simply copying and pasting what you wrote in the recommendation and click on "Recommend this person" on my profile at http://www.linkedin.com/in/jullien.

Thank you in advance,

Jullien Gordon

**EXAMPLE OF LINKEDIN.COM RECOMMENDATION FOR ANOTHER PERSON FROM YOU**

Considering my entrepreneurial path, I've only had one real boss in my adult career and that was Nicole Jones. I couldn't have asked for a better match.

1. She gave me room to create value.
2. She valued me as a person and employee.
3. She never made me compromise my values.

Even though she was my boss, I felt like an intrapreneur (or entrepreneuriial employee) because of the trust we cultivated. She gave me everything I needed to succeed including resources and directions, but she also gave me room to make mistakes and learn.

I felt as if I were working with her rather than for her—that's how I like to lead and be led. If I weren't doing my own thing, I would gladly work for Nicole again.

## 2.6 HOW TO CREATE PROFESSIONAL BUSINESS CARDS CHEAPLY

You're probably asking yourself, "Why would I need a business card if I'm still a student, and I don't have or work for a business yet?" Well, when you're networking with professionals who are where you want to be, business cards are the primary way professionals exchange information. Personal business cards demonstrate your professionalism, even if you don't have a profession yet.

Your business card should include the following information:
• Full name
• School e-mail address
• Primary phone number
• School name, graduation year, and major
• Optional: Web address
• Optional: Career aspiration (e.g., aspiring consultant)

Your business card can be used for personal and professional purposes. You can give it to new friends, a beautiful guy or girl you meet at a party, or a classmate with whom you want to form a study group. Professionally, they are great for networking events, career fairs, and any other interaction involving professionals.

You never know when you're going to meet someone who can help you or that you can help, so it's always good to have a few business cards on you. A card creates a smoother exchange of information than looking for a paper bag to rip and asking people walking by for a pen. That looks tacky and desperate to someone you are trying to impress.

When you're meeting people who can open doors for you, giving your business card first is the best way to get other people's business cards. It's more difficult to ask for a business card in the middle of a conversation than it is to reach in your pocket and offer your business card to someone. By habit, they will likely reciprocate the gesture without even saying anything.

Once you have someone's contact information, it's your responsibility to follow up and move the relationship forward by offering value when and where you can.

In this section, we're going to outline how you can create professional business cards cheaply.

## BUSINESS CARDS

### Directions:

1. Go to http://www.vistaprint.com or http://www.moo.com.
2. At Vistaprint.com select "Free Products" > "Free Business Cards".
3. Model your card using the exact same template and fields shown.
4. Get 250 cards for free. Pay only shipping & handling ($5.67 for 21-day delivery or about $10 for 14 days).

# 2.7 HOW TO CREATE PROFESSIONAL HEAD SHOTS AT HOME

Did you know that Facebook is the #1 photo sharing platform on the Internet? Your pictures are some of your most valuable possessions, and now many of them are online. It's great to get tagged in that old high school photo that you lost a long time ago. On the flip side, however, it's not so great to find yourself tagged doing inappropriate things at a fraternity party and then get 78 comments. Everything that gets posted about you on the web is not in your control, but it's important to upkeep what you can and one place to start is with your photos.

Your profile picture on Facebook, LinkedIn, your own website, and elsewhere can speak volumes about your professionalism. Granted, Facebook is for friends and fun, and LinkedIn is for business, but when it comes time to build relationships, people are going to search for you on the Internet, and they will care more about the content they find than the context they find it in.

The facts are that:
- 79 percent of employers now conduct an online search of applicants.
- Fully seventy percent say they have turned down applicants because of what they found online.
- Only 7 percent of job applicants were concerned about their online reputations.

One simple way to establish professionalism on the Internet is by having a good head shot. A great head shot can be taken by a professional photographer, but a good headshot can also be taken by a friend using a simple digital camera.

In this section, you will learn how to take a good professional photo that you can use to improve your online reputation.

**HEAD SHOTS**

**Directions:**
1. Find a digital camera, an inside setting with a plain wall or office environment, a sunny spot with no foot traffic, and a friend.
2. Find, clean, and iron a business outfit and a casual outfit and do your best to replicate the shots and angles below.
3. Take your business photo inside with a plain wall or an office-like background.
4. Take your casual photo outside with a hint of nature in the background.

**CASUAL PHOTOS**

# 2.8 HOW TO WRITE THE WORLD'S BEST RÉSUMÉ

You can write the most thorough résumé with strong action verbs, the nicest layout, and a record of the best schools and GPA, and print it on the finest paper, but if it doesn't communicate that you create value, the chances of you getting hired is slim.

**Size does matter.**
The sizing of each section of the résumé, is extremely important: 80 percent of your résumé is about your performance and 20 percent is about your personality. A lot of résumés are full of fluff. If you are overcompensating by filling up your résumé with achievements and awards from high school or words typed per minute, it's probably a sign that the size of your impact isn't that great. Where you went to school and your GPA don't matter as much as they used to—even a 4.0 won't get you hired today. The baseline is that you have finished college, created value, and led a group of people.

**Your résumé should not be a carbon copy of the job description.**
Most people simply find their current job description, copy and paste it into their résumé, and think they are done. Wrong! Most people's bullet points shoot them in the foot during the hiring process because they focus on responsibilities instead of results. Here are some examples of weak bullets:

* Led the sales team for our leading product and managed a team of 15 people.
* Completed weekly product reports to evaluate performance and progress.
* Supervised and trained 40 new staff members for the sales division.
* Led weekly staff meetings focused on employee development.

These bullets only speak to responsibilities—they don't communicate the value you created. Instead, each bullet-point should communicate how you moved the organization or some aspect of it from Point A to Point B. Potential employers are more concerned with what you moved forward than what you did back then. You should take it one step further and create a **Résumé 2.0 (See Module 2.11)**, which is more like a visual portfolio of your value. An addendum to your portfolio should include physical examples of the quality of your work (e.g., business plans or essays you've written, presentations you've created, an actual website or product you designed or marketed, etc.).

**The #1 thing you want to communicate is that you create value.**
**Value** is that which causes a transaction. True value forces whoever is being offered the value to make a choice. It causes the exchange or movement of time, money, and other forms of capital. Most people are indifferent and happy with who they are and where they are even though they may say they aren't. Value makes them admit that they want to be somewhere else, somewhere better, and that helps them actually get there.

107

A résumé speaks to the patterns of behavior you will resume at your new job and the #1 thing to communicate is that you create value wherever you go. If you've worked at a place for more than a year and can't speak to how you created change in that organization, then I wouldn't hire you. The sad thing is that people do great things in their organizations, but for some reason they don't effectively communicate it on their résumés. Wherever your next job is, you need pertinent points that communicate the value you created while you were there.

I call this the **Point A-to-B Résumé**. The basic premise is to address how you moved your last organization and/or yourself from Point A (where it was when you got there) to Point B (where it is when you leave). That's how value is created. The bullets for the same résumé as above using the Point A-to-B résumé model would look as follows:

**Point A to B Résumé Bullet Example**

| | |
|---|---|
| VERB: | Pioneered |
| WHAT: | a Go Green Save Green recycling program |
| POINT A: | decreasing our waste |
| POINT B: | by half |
| ACTION: | by leveraging video conferencing for regional meetings |

**Point A-to-B Bullets**
1. Built a sales team of 5 to 15 and increased the market share of our leading product by 10%.
2. Established an online accountability process to evaluate weekly progress.
3. Created a sales training curriculum that increased retention rates and first year sales of 40 new employees.

| BULLET | POINT A | POINT B |
|---|---|---|
| #1 | team of 5 | team of 15 |
| #1 | market share of N% | N+10% |
| #2 | no accountability process | online accountability process |
| #3 | N% retention rate | N% retention rate |
| #3 | $N first year sales | $N first year sales |

The best source of content for your résumé is probably in your quarterly or yearly evaluations from your boss—not your job description. A lot of times it just means thinking deeper about what you did and rephrasing what you already have. If you didn't create any value at your last organization, then you're in trouble. Why would a potential employer want someone who didn't create any value at their last job? The Point A to Point B résumé will be more effective at getting you the job you desire than the traditional job description-based résumé.

**Unemployment is caused by bad résumés, not a bad economy.**
Unemployment is not a sign of the lack of jobs in the economy. Unemployment is a sign of a lack of people who have and can demonstrate that they have created value for others in the past. That's why 80 percent of workers are underemployed, meaning that that they have jobs, but they aren't using their passion, they aren't reaching their full potential, and they aren't making their highest contribution to the world every day. Whereas the national unemployment rate is only 10 percent, underemployment is eight times that. This cycle starts with your résumé.

So many people drive to work, leave half themselves in the car, and drag the other half of themselves into the office. Note that underemployment has nothing to do with one's salary—You can be making $200,000 a year and still be underemployed. Economies fail when too many people are underemployed. Employees get mad when companies cut dead-weight and employers get mad when they realize that they hired dead weight. Are you dead weight or are you helping your company soar? It's hard for dead weight to move, as it simply holds on as long as it can.

**It is what it is.**
At the end of the day, a Résumé 1.0 won't get you a job and a Résumé 2.0 might land you an interview. A résumé is exactly what it means…without the accent (') over the two e's. It's a document that employers use to answer the question "Will this person be able to resume (pronounced re-zoom) their past success here?" But if you haven't been creating value where you are right now—even if you hate it—it's going to be difficult to communicate your value to another potential employer. If you hate your job, remember that you chose it by way of your past choices and actions which ultimately shaped your future choices. So seek to create value wherever you are because it will only position you to do things that you truly value in the near future.

## POINT A -TO-B RESUME BULLETS

**Directions:** Think of four personal or professional achievements that you are proud of and write them out using the Point A to B résumé bullet format below.

### Résumé Bullet #1

| | |
|---|---|
| VERB: | |
| WHAT: | |
| POINT A: | |
| POINT B: | |
| ACTION: | |

### Résumé Bullet #2

| | |
|---|---|
| VERB: | |
| WHAT: | |
| POINT A: | |
| POINT B: | |
| ACTION: | |

### Résumé Bullet #3

| | |
|---|---|
| VERB: | |
| WHAT: | |
| POINT A: | |
| POINT B: | |
| ACTION: | |

### Résumé Bullet #4

| | |
|---|---|
| VERB: | |
| WHAT: | |
| POINT A: | |
| POINT B: | |
| ACTION: | |

**SAMPLE RESUME**

**Directions:** Complete the sample resume template below to the best of your ability given what you have achieved personally and professionally so far.

Name:................................................................................................................

Mailing Address:................................................................................................

Phone:.................................................... E-mail:...........................................

15 Second Pitch:................................................................................................

........................................................................................................................

Long-Term Career Objective:.............................................................................

........................................................................................................................

Short-Term Career Objective:............................................................................

**Education**

College:.................................................... Degree:.......................................

Major:...................................................... Grad Date:....................................

High School:............................................ Grad Date:....................................

**Employment**

Company:................................................ Position:........................................

City:......................................................... Dates:...........................................

#1 Achievement:................................................................................................

#2 Achievement:................................................................................................

Company:................................................ Position:........................................

City:......................................................... Dates:...........................................

#1 Achievement:................................................................................................

#2 Achievement:................................................................................................

**Leadership & Volunteering**

Organization:............................................... Position:...................................................

City:.......................................................... Dates:......................................................

#1 Achievement:.............................................................................................................

Organization:............................................... Position:...................................................

City:.......................................................... Dates:......................................................

#1 Achievement:.............................................................................................................

Organization:............................................... Position:...................................................

City:.......................................................... Dates:......................................................

#1 Achievement:.............................................................................................................

**Top Hard Skills**

....................................................      ....................................................

....................................................      ....................................................

**Top Soft Skills**

....................................................      ....................................................

....................................................      ....................................................

**Awards & Honors**

.........................................................................................................................................

.........................................................................................................................................

.........................................................................................................................................

**Personal Interests & Hobbies**

.........................................................................................................................................

## 13 Cs OF RÉSUMÉ BULLET WRITING

**Directions:** Write 1-2 résumé bullet points for each of the 13Cs of Résumé Bullet Writing.

**1. Customer or Consumer:** Write 1-2 bullet points about how you moved a metric related to customers from Point A to Point B (e.g., loyalty, satisfaction, dollars per purchase, net promoter score, etc.).

..................................................................................................................

..................................................................................................................

..................................................................................................................

..................................................................................................................

**2. Cash Flow:** Write 1-2 bullet points about how you moved a metric related to cash flow from Point A to Point B (e.g., increased inflow, decreased outflow, etc.).

..................................................................................................................

..................................................................................................................

..................................................................................................................

..................................................................................................................

**3. Company:** Write 1-2 bullet points about how you moved a metric related to the company from Point A to Point B (e.g., rankings in best places to work, # of new clients, labor standards, decrease percent of defective products & returns, etc.).

..................................................................................................................

..................................................................................................................

..................................................................................................................

..................................................................................................................

**4. Colleagues:** Write 1-2 bullet points about how you moved a metric related to your colleagues from Point A to Point B (e.g., retention increase, on-board time decrease, grew full-time-equivalents (FTE) increase, number of mentorship relationships established, number of 360-degree feedback sessions completed, increased percent who participated in company retreat, increase in job security, etc.).

.......................................................................................................................................

.......................................................................................................................................

.......................................................................................................................................

.......................................................................................................................................

**5. Community:** Write 1-2 bullet points about how you moved a metric related to the community from Point A to Point B (e.g., number of hours volunteered, amount of matching funds, number of mentorships, dollar amounts of pro bono work, etc.).

.......................................................................................................................................

.......................................................................................................................................

.......................................................................................................................................

.......................................................................................................................................

**6. Capital:** Write 1-2 bullet points about how you moved a metric related to the capital from Point A to Point B (e.g., increase in assets, decrease in debt, mergers, acquisitions, division sold, financing raised, etc.).

.......................................................................................................................................

.......................................................................................................................................

.......................................................................................................................................

.......................................................................................................................................

**7. Culture:** Write 1-2 bullet points about how you moved a metric related to the company culture from Point A to Point B (e.g., increased employee satisfaction, number of innovative projects, employee safety rating, etc.).

.......................................................................................................................................

.......................................................................................................................................

.......................................................................................................................................

**8. Campaign:** Write 1-2 bullet points about how you moved a metric related to an internal or external campaign from Point A to Point B (e.g., page views, conversion rate, media impressions, subscribers, etc.).

..................................................................................................................................

..................................................................................................................................

..................................................................................................................................

..................................................................................................................................

**9. Champion of Change:** Write 1-2 bullet points about how you moved a metric related to a change you led from Point A to Point B (e.g., carbon emissions decrease, switched software & executed national training, shifted market from computers to consulting, etc.).

..................................................................................................................................

..................................................................................................................................

..................................................................................................................................

..................................................................................................................................

**10. Communication:** Write 1-2 bullet points about how you moved a metric related to the company communication from Point A to Point B (e.g., integrated a CMS, established meeting process and protocol, created a Wiki to share intelligence, etc.).

..................................................................................................................................

..................................................................................................................................

..................................................................................................................................

..................................................................................................................................

**11. Competition:** Write 1-2 bullet points about how you moved a metric related to the competition from Point A to Point B (e.g., passed Toyota for #1 spot, increased market share by 10%, competition closed 5 stores in new market, etc.).

..................................................................................................................................

..................................................................................................................................

..................................................................................................................................

..................................................................................................................................

**12. Collaboration:** Write 1-2 bullet points about how you moved a metric related to collaboration or partnerships from Point A to Point B (e.g., built new supplier relationship, landed $100K sponsorship, led cross-divisional team to create new product, etc.).

...................................................................................................................

...................................................................................................................

...................................................................................................................

...................................................................................................................

**13. Concepts:** Write 1-2 bullet points about how you moved a metric related to concepts you created from Point A to Point B (e.g., created a new business line that grew to $4M, revamped lead generation process using my 4Ps framework, etc.).

...................................................................................................................

...................................................................................................................

...................................................................................................................

...................................................................................................................

## OTHER METRICS TO MENTION

**Financial:** Measures the economic impact of actions on growth, profitability and risk from the shareholder's perspective (net income, ROI, ROA, cash flow).

**Customer:** Measures the ability of an organization to provide quality goods and services that meet customer expectations (customer retention, profitability, satisfaction and loyalty).

**Internal Business Processes:** Measures the internal business processes that create customer and shareholder satisfaction (project management, total quality management, Six Sigma).

**Learning and Growth:** Measures the organizational environment that fosters change, innovation, information, sharing, and growth (staff morale, training, knowledge sharing).

**Productivity:** Measures employee output (units/ transactions/dollars), the uptime levels, and how employees use their time (sales-to-assets ratio, dollar revenue from new customers, sales pipeline).

**Quality:** Measures the ability to meet and/or exceed the requirements and expectations of the customer (customer complaints, percent returns, defects per million opportunities or DPMO).

**Profitability:** Measures the overall effectiveness of the management organization in generating profits (profit contribution by segment/customer, margin spreads).

**Timeliness:** Measures the point in time (day/week/ month) when management and employee tasks are completed (on-time delivery, percent of late orders).

**Process Efficiency:** Measures how effectively the management organization incorporates quality control, Six Sigma, and best practices to streamline operational processes (yield percentage, process uptime, capacity utilization).

**Activity Time:** Measures the duration of time (hours/days/months) required by employees to complete tasks (processing time, time to service customer).

**Resource Utilization:** Measures how effectively the management organization leverages existing business resources such as assets, bricks and mortar, investments (sales per total assets, sales per channel, win rate).

**Cost Savings:** Measures how successfully the management organization achieves economies of scale and scope of work with its people, staff, and practices to control operational and overhead costs (cost per unit, inventory turns, cost of goods).

**Growth:** Measures the ability of the management organization to maintain competitive economic position in the growth of the economy and industry (market share, customer acquisition/retention, account penetration).

**Innovation:** Measures the capability of the organization to develop new products, processes, and services to penetrate new markets and customer segments (new patents, new product rollouts, R&D spending).

**Technology:** Measures how effectively the IT organization develops, implements, and maintains information management infrastructure and applications (IT capital spending, CRM technologies implemented, Web-enabled access).

# 2.9 HOW TO THINK, TALK, & ACT LIKE YOU ALREADY WORK THERE

Before the interview, you also want to understand the industry and business model of the company you hope to work for. Interviewing isn't just about seeing how nice you are—it's to determine whether or not you will be valuable to the potential employer. Measuring your value comes down to a single question: "Will you create more value for the company than you take in the form of a salary?"

The potential employer isn't going to hire you just because you have a good GPA and a good personality. Your GPA may be correlated to future performance, but the work world and school world are two different games. Keep in mind that hiring is a risk—it's an investment in someone they don't fully know yet. Therefore, your goal in the interview is to take as much risk out of the equation for them as possible.

Consider how the first job ever got created. The potential employee didn't walk up to an entrepreneur and say "Here's where I went to school" or "People think I'm nice." He walked up to an entrepreneur and either said "I have an idea for you." or "I can help your business grow and here's how." Unemployment isn't a function of people being incapable of doing the work—it's a function of people not knowing their value and/or being incapable of communicating their value to potential employers in a compelling way. In some cases, people haven't created any true value beyond their academic achievements and that's not enough to guarantee gainful employment.

A great question to ask yourself is "What am I proud of?" Is there something—anything—that you've done in your life that helped someone else that you can say you are truly proud of? If not, then why not? If not, then create something if you want financial abundance in your life. The best way to become a millionaire is to help other people become millionaires.

Let's say you want to make $50,000 per year. If that's the case, somehow, throughout the entire interview process, you have to convince the potential employer that you will create at least $75,000 in value for the company. That way they keep $25,000 and you take $50,000. Your tools of persuasion include your past performance, your leadership, and other experiences. Another good question to ask yourself is: "If were CEO of a company, how much would I pay myself...honestly?" When you put yourself in their shoes, you start to see salary and yourself differently.

In order to figure out how you can help a company make more money or save more money, you have to understand how they make money now. This is called their **business model**. You don't have to have an MBA to understand how a company makes money. Here's a framework that will help called the **Average Business Cycle** (ABCs of Business).

# The Average Business Cycle

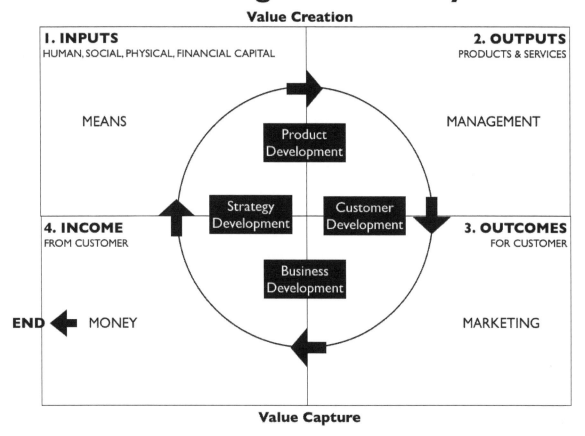

**Inputs:** It's impossible for a business to begin without some sort of capital—even if it is sweat equity from a founding entrepreneur, a business requires something to start. All businesses perform some sort of alchemy because they combine capital A and capital B to create new capital C with the hopes of earning more capital M (money). The four forms of capital include human, social, physical, and financial capital.

Human capital includes employees, but more importantly how they spend their time. You can have thousands of employees, but if they don't spend their time in a way that ultimately creates more capital M, then the business won't last long.

Social capital includes personal, professional, or political relationships. Relationships that help a business could be with buyers, distributors, manufacturers, sellers of parts, lawmakers, middlemen, banks, investors, or key employees and experts.

Physical capital includes raw materials and physical space. Raw materials could be aluminum, cotton, seeds, plastic, water, and land, among other things. Physical space has to do with offices, stores, warehouses, and distribution centers. Physical space and the access to physical resources can determine the success or failure of a business, that's why a company like McDonald's strives to control the production of potatoes and reproduction of cows as well as buy real estate on the world's busiest corners.

Financial capital includes assets, investments, credit, and access to money or discounts that can fuel a business's growth. Two entrepreneurs can have the same idea at the same time, but perhaps the one who can get the financial capital needed to grow the business can grow it faster by giving up equity in exchange for financial capital instead of building the business on sweat equity alone. On the savings side, a business like USPS doesn't have to pay for physical space because the government usually gives it to them, and they don't have to pay federal taxes which gives them an advantage because their competitors (such as UPS or FedEx) do.

**Outputs:** Outputs are the results of product or service development processes which involve combining capital A and capital B to create new capital C. Other words for outputs are products or services. Products or services are the ways that businesses help customers get to their desired outcome(s). Outputs are a function of your inputs— one change in inputs and you may have a completely different business.

**Outcomes:** Outcomes are what customers really buy, not a business's outputs. A hammer and nail are nice, but the outcome I bought them for was a picture of my friends on my wall. If customers believe that your product or service will help them achieve their desired outcome with more certainty, more speed, and more savings than a competitor, that increases the likelihood that they will buy from you versus someone else. This is the primary goal of customer development.

Customers may derive an outcome from a product or service that the business didn't intend when it created the product or service. For instance, Apple makes computers and phones to help customers create, sync, and share media easier. However, there are some customers who have bought iPhones and iPads simply because they are cool, not because the customer wants to create. This is great for Apple, and it also proves the point that people buy outcomes, not outputs. In this case, some people were buying "coolness" versus the ability to create.

**Income:** Income is what is left over when the business subtracts all of its expenses from its revenues. Revenues are generated when customers pay for new capital C with capital M. Expenses include the expenses related to all of the inputs (human, social, physical, and financial) plus expenses associated with the alchemy of turning capital A and capital B into new capital C and the cost of making the customer aware that new capital C is available and getting it to them where they can pay for it.

Once a business has a product or service, customers become aware of it and can access it. Business development is the process of causing a transaction or exchange of new capital C for capital M. Inputs and outputs make up the value creation process. Outcomes and income make up the value capture process.

There are two types of companies that go out of business:
1. Ones that don't create any value.
2. Ones that create value but aren't able to capture enough of it to sustain themselves.

A business can have an amazing product or service but the wrong business model to sustain its growth. Good businesses capture enough of the value they create to keep the business cycle going. Through the sales process, businesses have to convince competitors' customers that their product or service is better. An example of this situation would be millions of people leaving Myspace.com for Facebook.com. Otherwise, they have to convince **non-customers** (people who don't currently spend money on products or services similar to the ones they offer) that their products or services actually help the customer achieve an existing outcome in an easier way than what they may have already been reaching. An example of this situation would be fast food restaurants convincing mothers that there is an easier way to feed their families than buying groceries and cooking, or going out for dinner. It may not be healthier, but it's easier than cooking.

When a business changes the way customers spends their personal income, the business generates income. Some of that income goes back to investors and to service debt. The rest of it goes back into the business to continue to improve the business cycle by closing gaps and limiting inefficiencies. For instance, if the biggest challenge in the business model involves customer development and awareness, then a company might invest in a brand manager, social media expert, marketing director, or distribution partnerships to accelerate the cycle. If the company believes that its business cycle is perfect, then it may just want to increase all of the inputs and do the exact same thing on a larger scale until it doesn't work, or the company sees a great opportunity to use what they have to do something different.

This discussion about the Average Business Cycle should help you to understand the basic business cycle of your desired industry or company and thus show you how the job you are applying for fits within the organization. Once you know where you fit, you will better understand how you could contribute to the value creation and value capture process, giving you an edge on those who simply thought the job looked appealing.

This kind of understanding may not be as relevant for big companies with established hiring processes, but according the U.S. Bureau of Labor Statistics, small organizations (1-250 employees) employ 66 percent of the American workforce while medium organizations (250-1000 employees) employ 18 percent; large organizations (1000+ employees) employ only 16 percent. These statistics mean that the greatest opportunities for you may be in smaller organizations rather than just the big ones that recruit on campus.

**Directions:** Consider the Average Business Cycle for your target industry or company, and define the inputs, outputs, outcomes, and income that typical companies in your industry seek to produce.

| | WHAT ARE THE KEY METRICS FOR THIS INDUSTRY/ COMPANY? |
|---|---|
| **INPUTS**<br>- HUMAN RESOURCES<br>- FINANCIAL RESOURCES<br>- PHYSICAL RESOURCES | 1 |
| | 2 |
| | 3 |
| **OUTPUTS**<br>- PRODUCTS<br>- SERVICES | 1 |
| | 2 |
| | 3 |
| **OUTCOMES**<br>- RESULTS FOR CUSTOMER | 1 |
| | 2 |
| | 3 |
| **INCOME**<br>- CASH<br>- BRAND<br>- ETC. | 1 |
| | 2 |
| | 3 |

**Directions:** Use your understanding of your target industry's inputs, outputs, outcomes, and income to determine how your passions, skills, and strengths can help a company increase or decrease their metrics.

| | HOW CAN YOU INCREASE/DECREASE THESE METRICS? |
|---|---|
| **INPUTS**<br>- HUMAN RESOURCES<br>- FINANCIAL RESOURCES<br>- PHYSICAL RESOURCES | 1 |
| | 2 |
| | 3 |
| **OUTPUTS**<br>- PRODUCTS<br>- SERVICES | 1 |
| | 2 |
| | 3 |
| **OUTCOMES**<br>- RESULTS FOR CUSTOMER | 1 |
| | 2 |
| | 3 |
| **INCOME**<br>- CASH<br>- BRAND<br>- ETC. | 1 |
| | 2 |
| | 3 |

## AVERAGE BUSINESS CYCLE

**Directions:** Fill in the four quadrants of the Average Business Cycle for your target industry or company by writing in the inputs, outputs, outcomes, and income. Ask someone in that industry or company for feedback to ensure accuracy.

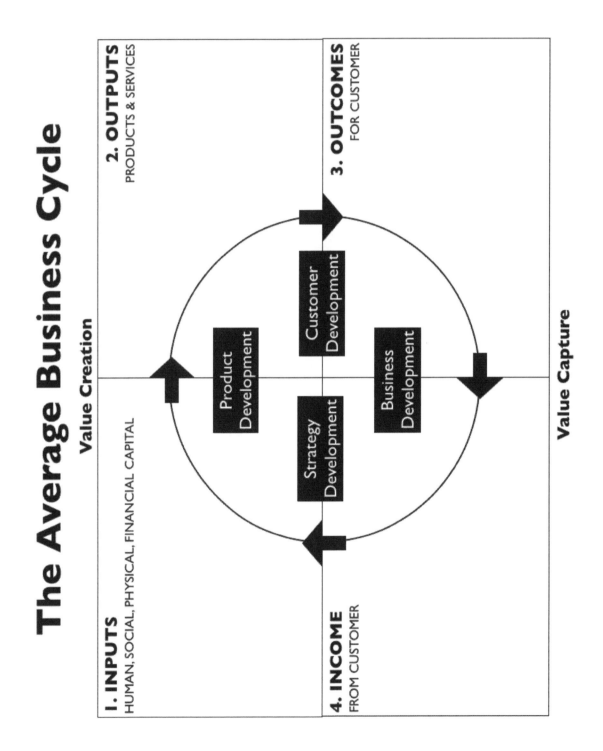

# The Average Business Cycle

**Value Creation**

**2. OUTPUTS**
PRODUCTS & SERVICES

**3. OUTCOMES**
FOR CUSTOMER

**1. INPUTS**
HUMAN, SOCIAL, PHYSICAL, FINANCIAL CAPITAL

**4. INCOME**
FROM CUSTOMER

**Value Capture**

- Product Development
- Customer Development
- Strategy Development
- Business Development

# 2.10 HOW TO WRITE A GREAT COVER LETTER

A great cover letter contextualizes (but doesn't copy) your résumé. In the same way that your 30 second pitch may be different based on who you are meeting and where you are meeting them, your cover letter puts your résumé into context based on the specific job and company of interest.

|  | **COVER LETTER** | **RÉSUMÉ** |
|---|---|---|
| Purpose | To position and connect you using your assessment of fit | To prove your credibility by describing your past performance |
| Form | Story in paragraphs | Specifics in bullets |

Your cover letter can introduce your résumé in a way that builds the bridge for a potential employer and tells the brief story of why this is the most logical next move for you and them. For instance, let's say a candidate has extensive academic experience in mathematics, and the company wants to explore marketing. A sample cover letter sentence based on this person's background may be:

"Millions of marketing dollars are wasted on trying to reach the masses, when statistical analysis can reveal who the most valuable customers are and focus the company's efforts on reaching them."

This sentence closes the gap for the cover letter reader between mathematics and marketing and shows why mathematics is extremely important to the company's business model.

You're trying to make your case for hire. You are trying to convince the judge (ultimate decision maker) and the jury (employees you interview with) that you are guilty of being the best fit for this job and this company. Your cover letter serves as your main argument and your résumé provides the supporting evidence. In order to win the case, you have to relate to them, speak in their language, and answer up front any anticipated questions—stated and unstated—they may have about your candidacy.

Every cover letter you write should be customized based on the position and the company. In this section, we're going to draft a general cover letter that you can adjust based on your self-understanding and understanding of the job and company.

## COVER LETTERS

**Directions:** Use the template below to create a typed draft of your general cover letter which will be customized for each job you apply for.

## COVER LETTER EXAMPLE

E-MAIL SUBJECT: Dear Mr./Mrs. Hiring Manager, Referred by Mr. Big Shot

John Smith
1000 Hire Me Way
New York, NY 10001
john@johnsmith.com
(310) 353-2432

March 1, 2011

Employer Name
Address
City, State, Zip

Dear Mr./Mrs. Hiring Manager:

**1st Paragraph**

I am interested in applying for the *summer internship program* opportunity
PROGRAM OR POSITION NAME

that I discovered through *Daryn Smith, Chief Marketing Officer at INC*
NAME & POSITION OR PERSON & PLACE

Currently I'm a *sophomore at Indiana University majoring in business*
YOUR YEAR, SCHOOL, & MAJOR

and I'm seeking professional experiences that will position me to pursue a full-time

career working *in consumer products marketing*
IN INDUSTRY, AS FUNCTION, OR WITH TARGET MARKET

upon graduating in *Spring 2014*
SEMESTER AND YEAR

**2nd Paragraph**

My unique ability to.. *identify what motivates people to take action* ..............
MOST RELEVANT SUPER POWER

especially as it relates to... *millennials and their spending patterns* ..............
INDUSTRY, FUNCTION, OR TARGET MARKET

makes me the ideal candidate for the job. I have a deep passion for

.................. *creating content that helps people succeed* ..............
YOUR PASSION

and like .............. *Top Gun Employment* ..............I am committed to
COMPANY NAME

solving the problem OR answering the question of..............

.............. *underemployment and unemployment* ..............
THE PROBLEM THE COMPANY OR POSITION ADDRESS

because I believe that . *millennials, and all people for that matter* ..............
CUSTOMERS, ORGANIZATION, OR PEOPLE IN GENERAL

deserve to OR should experience what it means to OR have a right to OR

.. *be fully employed, make their highest contribution, and create value* ..............
YOUR POSSIBILITY OR PICTURE

**3rd Paragraph**

I would appreciate an invitation for a formal interview or an informational interview to learn more about this position, the problem it is supposed to solve, and its success metrics as they relate to the company's strategy. That way, we can accurately assess together my fit for the position.

I have attached my résumé for your consideration. I welcome the chance to speak to you soon and will follow up via phone in a week or so if that is convenient.

Sincerely,

..... *Jullien Gordon* ..............
YOUR NAME

# 2.11 HOW TO SET YOURSELF APART WITH A RÉSUMÉ 2.0 OR PORTFOLIO

Before higher education was so prominent, jobs would come about via relationships. Once higher education became more established, the key to getting a good job was relationships and relevant education. In today's economy, the way to get a good job after college involves relationships, relevant education, and results.

Employers see you as a risk until proven otherwise, and the best proof is your results of value creation. Every company is hiring, even in an economic downturn. In other words, no company is not hiring. When a company is down, it will hire anyone it thinks will take it higher. The only way to bounce back from an economic downturn is to either lay off people and hope that things return to the good ol' days, or hire great people who will be **intrapreneurs**—employees who think and act like entrepreneurs—and think of new ways to reposition and repurpose the company through innovation.

If someone great knocks on the door, the company won't shut it. However, keep in mind that I don't mean great as in great person or personality—I mean someone with a great performance track record. Nice people don't always produce nice results. It's sad but true that personality and performance aren't correlated. Personality gets you only so far. Sometimes nice guys finish last because they don't perform.

Have you created extreme value? If so, how? Your text-based Résumé 1.0 can't fully communicate your true value. You have to shift from telling via your résumé and interview to showing. Anybody can talk the talk, but can you walk the walk? The more you show, the more convinced they will be of your value.

A **Résumé 2.0** is a portfolio of your best work. Think of your Résumé 1.0 as your table of contents and your Résumé 2.0 as the actual evidence. Your Résumé 2.0 can include documents such as:
* academic work,
* a professional or volunteer project,
* marketing materials from an event you organized,
* a PowerPoint you created on a topic of passion,
* writing samples (e.g., white paper, article, blog post, speech),
* a product you worked on,
* pictures of other relevant results.

Tangible results are always more convincing than talked-about results. Whatever evidence you can't show on your résumé should be in your Résumé 2.0.

Even though you just wrote a résumé, the résumé 1.0 breed is dying. A single sheet of paper with text can't capture who you are. However, perhaps you don't want to develop a full website either. So, the best way to introduce yourself to potential employers is with a Résumé 2.0. Show. Don't tell. No need to say much more. A great Résumé 2.0 speaks for itself.

## RESUME 2.0

### Directions:
1. View a sample résumé 2.0 at http://www.innerviewing.me/resume20.
2. Download the résumé 2.0 template at http://www.innerviewing.me/resume20.
3. Create a www.Slideshare.net account.
4. Create your résumé 2.0 using the template and table of contents below.
5. Upload your résumé 2.0 to Slideshare.net.
6. Get the embed code & add it to your website.

## TABLE OF CONTENTS

**THE INTRO**
SLIDE 1 TITLE: NAME & PROFESSIONAL PICTURE
SLIDE 2 TITLE: TABLE OF CONTENTS & INTENTION
SLIDE 3 TITLE: 30 SECOND PITCH

**THE PAST**
SLIDE 4 TITLE: LIFELONG LEARNER (=FORMAL & INFORMAL EDUCATION)
SLIDE 5 TITLE: LIFELONG LEADER
SLIDE 6 TITLE: PERSONAL ASSETS (=PASSIONS, SKILLS, & STRENGTHS)
SLIDE 7 TITLE: #1 ASSET WITH MULTIPLE EXAMPLES
SLIDE 8 TITLE: COMPANY #1 & VALUE CREATED THERE
SLIDE 9 TITLE: COMPANY #2 & VALUE CREATED THERE

**THE PRESENT**
SLIDE 10 TITLE: MY PASSIONS, PROBLEMS, POSITIONING, & PURPOSE
SLIDE 11 TITLE: _____ (ROLE #2 & #3 E.G., FAMILY MAN, SOCCER COACH)
SLIDE 12 TITLE: PAST OR PRESENT PROJECTS
SLIDE 13 TITLE: DASHBOARD FOR SUCCESS
SLIDE 14 TITLE: SUCCESS SYSTEMS & ORGANIZATIONAL AFFILIATIONS (E.G., 30 DAY DO IT GROUP, MASTERMIND GROUP, CHURCH, MENTORS, PROFESSIONAL ORGANIZATIONS, TRAININGS)

**THE FUTURE**
SLIDE 15 TITLE: THREE PERSONAL & PROFESSIONAL GOALS
SLIDE 16 TITLE: VISION (=VISION BOARD, EULOGY, OR RETIREMENT SPEECH)
SLIDE 17 TITLE: CONTACT INFORMATION

**ADDENDUM ITEMS (Convert documents to PDFs using** http://www.freepdfconvert.com**)**

- Business Plan
- Academic Work
- Professional Project
- Volunteer Project
- Extracurricular Activity
- Writing Sample (White Paper, Article, Blog Post, Speech)
- PowerPoint
- Pictures
- Flyers
- Products
- Screenshots

# 2.12 HOW TO CREATE A FREE WEBSITE THAT WOOS POTENTIAL EMPLOYERS

Facebook and LinkedIn let you customize only so much. Facebook fields are limited and LinkedIn restricts you to your online résumé. You need the freedom to display who you are the way you want without having to learn too much HTML. You need an online home that speaks for you when you aren't physically present to speak for yourself.

Having your own website allows you to customize how unknown visitors on the web—who could be potential employers—perceive you. People tend to think that someone's first impression of them occurs the first time they meet in person, but in this digital age, first impressions normally take place online when you're not there to represent yourself.

Your homepage is that home. It's like a welcome mat that invites people to come into your digital life and get to know more about you. Unlike LInkedIn, your website doesn't have to be solely professional. Also, unlike Facebook, your website doesn't have to be solely social. Your personal website serves as a combination of the two in addition to including your portfolio, Résumé 1.0, Résumé 2.0, headshot, blog entries, and other cool things that paint the full picture of who you are, what you're passionate about and why, in a way that social networks and social media can't.

Your website allows you to paint a holistic picture of who you are. Through your website, you can invite people into your living room through your 30 second pitch or your Résumé 2.0. Then you can offer them some food for thought via your blog where you share your passions and insights. You can show them your bedroom and shoebox of pictures. In addition, you can take them into your office by showing them your professional portfolio and Résumé 1.0. Finally, you can take them into your shed where your hobbies exist, whether they are sports, travel, or crafts.

Every home or apartment has its own character, and your homepage and website allow you to show yours and invite people in as much as you want. Below are a few examples of great personal and professional websites to model yours after.

**Great Examples of Personal Websites:**
http://www.julliengordon.weebly.com
http://www.socialjenny.com
http://tomwantsajob.wordpress.com
http://www.michaelboezi.com

# www.julliengordon.weebly.com

## JULLIEN GORDON

Home   Resume 1.0   Resume 2.0   Downloads   Blog   Contact

Jullien Gordon Resume 2.0

**Meet**
Jullien Gordon
**Purpose Finder**

View more presentations from Jullien Gordon.

## More About Me

I was born and raised in the San Francisco Bay Area where I graduated from Bishop O'Dowd High School with honors and as ASB Vice President. From there I went on to get my BA from UCLA (in 3 years) and two masters degrees from Stanford—my MBA and Masters in Education.

I'm a social butterfly with a cacoon. One side of me likes to be out meeting new people and breaking bread with friends and family. The other side of me likes to be alone and focused as I write and think of world changing ideas.

## My 30 Second Pitch

My name is Jullien Gordon and I'm a PurposeFinder. I help individuals and organization discover and align their lives with their purpose so that they can make their highest contribution in the world.

I have achieved amazing results with 1,000s of individuals and dozens of for-profit and non-profit organizations including Coburn Ventures, Management Leadership for Tomorrow, and the SHAPE Program.

**jullien_gordon_resume_cccp1.pdf**
Download File

---

**Jullien Gordon - Blog**

**The Problem with Personal Development Industry**
I've been study the personal development industry for quite some time now and I think that the game is changing and...

**The Recent Push toward Consolidation**
Lately, an interesting thing has been occurring in the personal development industry. Everyone has been consolidati...

**My Passion for Personal Development**
I remember creating my own weekly time grid using Microsoft Excel in junior high school. Little did I know that it ...

131

## CREATING A WEEBLY WEBSITE

### Setting up your Weebly.com Account

1. Go to http://www.weebly.com.

2. Enter your name, e-mail address, and a password to sign up.

3. Choose a site name.

4. Choose "Use a subdomain of Weebly.com."

### Choosing a Design

1. Now go back to www.weebly.com and click the design button in the header. Choose any theme and some sort of header image.

### Adding Content to your Homepage

1. Click on the header image and upload your professional photo.

If you would like the resize your header image to fit the entire box, click the header image to get the header image size and then go to http://www.resize.it. Click "Advanced Tools." Upload the image. Enter the pixels from the header. Click "Okay." Move the crop to where you want it. Click "Crop It." Right click the image and "Save as..." and then type "My Website Header."

2. Click "Elements" in the header.

3. Drag "Two Column Layout" under your header image.

4. In the box on the left, drag "Paragraph with Text."

5. Add the title "My 30 Second Pitch" and then paste your 30 second pitch here.

6. In the box on the right, drag "Custom HTML."

7. In the code, change the 425px to 330px.

### Embedding Multimedia

1. Get the embed code from Slideshare.net for your Résumé 2.0. Change width="425" height="355" to width="330" height="270" twice within the code.

2. Drag another "Two Column Layout" under your original one.

3. In the box on the left, drag "Paragraph with Text."

4. Add the title "More About Me" and add a short bio that speaks to where you're from, your education, your personality, the various roles you play and hats you wear, and how you spend your free time.

**Adding an RSS Feed**

1. In the box on the right, add an RSS Feed Reader by selecting "More" in the "Elements" tab and dragging "Feed Reader" into the box.

2. Click the box and for the "Feed Address" type in http://julliengordon.weebly.com/1/feed, except replace my name with your name.

**Creating New Pages**

1. Click the "Pages" tab.

2. Click the "New Page" button and title it "Résumé 1.0."

3. Click the "New Page" button and title it "Résumé 2.0."

4. Click the "New Blog" button and title it "Blog."

5. Click the "New Page" button and title it "Downloads."

6. Click the "New Page" button and title it "Contact."

7. Click the "Save" button.

**Integrating Your Résumé 1.0**

1. Click on the "Résumé 1.0" page.

2. Drag "Custom HTML" under the header.

3. Click on the box and click "Edit Custom HTML."

4. Paste this code in the box:

Go to <object data="http://docs.google.com/View?id=dc55sw65_970dm3pnzhd" width="700" height="2000"> <embed src="http://docs.google.com/View?id=dc55sw65_970dm3pnzhd" width="700" height="2000"> Error: Embedded data could not be displayed. </object>

5. Go to Google Docs (http://docs.google.com) and open up your résumé.

6. Click "File" and click "Make a copy."

7. Rename the document to "Résumé for Web."

8. Remove your mailing address (and phone number if you want) from the heading.

9. In the right hand corner click "Share" and select "Publish as a webpage."

10. Click "Publish document."

11. Copy the URL that appears after you click the button.

12. Check the "Automatically re-publish" box.

13. Go back to Weebly.com and replace http://docs.google.com/View?id=dc55sw65_970dm3pnzhd with your new URL in two places in the code.

14. Adjust the height from 2000 (in two places) to fit your résumé.

**Integrating Your Résumé 2.0**

1. Click on the "Résumé 2.0" page.

2. Drag "Custom HTML" under the header.

3. Click on the box and click "Edit Custom HTML."

4. Get the embed code from Slideshare.net for your Résumé 2.0. Change width="425" height="355" to width="700" height="585" twice within the code.

**Uploading Downloads**

1. Click on the "Downloads" page.

2. Click "More" which comes after "Multimedia" & "Revenue" in the "Elements" tab.

3. Drag "File" down two times.

4. In the first file, upload your Résumé 1.0.

5. In the second file, upload your Résumé 2.0.

6. Feel free to add more files that demonstrate the quality of your work.

**Adding Blog Entries**

1. Click on the "Blog" page just to see how it looks. We're going to come back to that later.

**Adding your Contact Information**

1. Click on the "Contact" page.

2. Drag "Paragraph with Title" under the header.

3. Title it "Feel free to say hello."

4. Paste the text below with your own information:

E-mail: john@johnsmith.com
Phone: 646-875-8342
LinkedIn: http://www.linkedin.com/in/johnsmith
Facebook: http://www.facebook.com/johnsmith
Twitter: http://www.twitter.com/johnsmith

# 2.13 HOW TO BUY WWW.YOURNAME.COM AND GET FIRSTNAME@YOURNAME.COM

Have you ever googled yourself? If not, you're not alone: 31 percent of people have never conducted a search on their own name using a search engine to learn what is visible to potential employers. If so, what comes up? Is it even you? Is it someone who shares your name but not your professionalism? Is it what you expect or not?

Most people have no clue about and no control over their online presence. Their online brand is limited to Facebook and the dozen other social media websites that they have joined, and social media sites aren't always the most professional. While you can establish privacy settings on sites like Facebook, the last thing you want a potential employer who googles you to find is an inappropriate profile picture, Facebook status update, or tweet.

Having your own domain name looks professional and allows you to create your own e-mail address that you can use after you graduate such as john@johnsmith.com. When you have your own e-mail address, it shows that you're ahead of the curve because most people don't have one. It shows that you're valuable and available (rather than giving out a company e-mail address that makes you look set), and it naturally invites people you meet to go to your website to see what's there and learn more about you.

Even if you don't choose to build a website, having your own domain name allows you to forward onlookers to a web page that best represents you whether that means forwarding them to LinkedIn.com, CareerScribe.com, BeyondCredentials.com, or About.me.

**BUYING YOUR DOMAIN NAME**

**Directions:**
1. Go to http://www.godaddy.com or any other domain name provider.
2. Try the following different combinations in case your preference is not available.

Examples:
www.julliengordon.com (Ideal)
www.julliengordon.org (.org instead of .com)
www.julliengordon.net (.net instead of .com)
www.julliengordon.me (.me instead of .com)
www.julliengordon.info (.info instead of .com)
www.julienngordon.com (middle initial)
www.jullien-gordon.com (add hyphen)
www.jgordon.com (first initial only)
www.jngordon.com (first and middle initial)
www.thejulliengordon.com (add the to the front)
www.julliengordoninc.com (add inc to the end)

3. Search for GoDaddy.com discount codes on RetailMeNot.com.
4. Purchase your domain name.

## E-MAIL FORWARDING

**Directions:**

1. Log in to your "Account Manager."

2. In the "My Products" section, click "E-mail."

3. Next to the account you want to use, click "Manage Account."

4. If you have unused e-mail plans, and have not previously disabled the pop-in message that displays, click "View All" to view your complete list of e-mail plans.

5. On the left, click "Forwarding Plans" to use a forwarding plan you have already set up, or click "Unused Forwarding", under the "Unused Plans" folder to use a new plan.

6. Click Add next to the "E-mail Forwarding" account you want to use.

7. Click Add for the forwarding account to which you want to add a forwarding address.

8. In the Add Forward field, enter the first part of the e-mail address, i.e., the user name.

9. In the "Forward Mail To" field, enter the e-mail address that you want to forward messages to.

10. To make the mailbox a catch-all account, select "Yes". A catch-all account receives all messages sent to non-existent e-mail addresses at your domain. For example, unknown@mydomain.com.

11. To set an automatic response for this account, select "Auto-Responder", and then type the message in the auto-responder message text box. You can also specify a date and time for the auto response to start and end. An auto-response allows you to automatically send a reply message to people who send you e-mail messages.

12. Click "OK."

**LINKING YOUR DOMAIN NAME TO WEEBLY.COM**

**Directions:**

1. Login to Weebly.com.

2. Go to your website and click the "Settings" tab.

3. Click "Change site address."

4. Select "Use a domain you already own" and type in your domain name.

5. Choose Option A, by copying and pasting the e-mail template provided and send it to your domain registrar or choose Option B, click "See instructions," and make the DNS change yourself.

For additional support look at: http://support.weebly.com/support/index.php?pg=kb.page&id=4 or call GoDaddy.com Support at (480) 505-8877.

# 2.14 HOW TO USE 3 SIMPLE & SHORT BLOGS TO SHOW YOU ARE COMPETENT

People blog for different reasons: for personal satisfaction (like a journal), for notoriety, to teach others, and to document and share their thoughts among many other reasons. In this case, we are going to use your blog to demonstrate your industry awareness and to position you as someone who has been thinking critically about this career and industry for a while beyond just your upcoming interview.

Blogging is a chance to tell your story in the context of your industry. Perhaps you never had to write a paper for a class on your target industry, or your major doesn't connect to your desired field of work at all. You probably still have innovative thoughts about your industry. You can show them in advance of your interview through blogging about why you are passionate about this career. You could also blog about a problem and solution you see that could change the industry if addressed and implemented.

Your passion, your articulation of the problems facing an industry, and your awareness of current events says a great deal about your preparedness. When someone lands on your website and sees that you are an original thinker, it speaks volumes without you talking. Employers want to know if you "get it," so writing your thoughts and sharing them publicly says a lot about your competency and communication skills.

Writing your thoughts down will also help you when networking. You can use your blogs as conversation starters. Further, because you've already processed your ideas through writing, you will sound more confident and thoughtful when you speak. Moreover, it will appear as if what you say is an original, in-the-moment thought, which makes you appear extremely smart.

In this next section, you are going to share some of your thoughts about your target industry using the templates provided. You can type directly into your Weebly.com blog (at http://www.weebly.com/weebly/main.php) instead of writing in the templates. By the time you're done, your blog will have at least three new entries and you will have successfully positioned yourself as a critical thinker in your field of interest.

**PASSION BLOG**

**Key Questions:**
- Why are you so passionate about this industry?
- When was the first time you realized this was your passion?
- What was your first influence? A book? A conference? A person? A website? An article? A television show? A movie? A person?
- How are you actively engaging your passion today?
- What are 5 things you would recommend that people who share your passion should check out?

**Entry Title: 5 Things You Must See If You Life [YOUR PASSION HERE]**

My passion for ................................................. began in ...............................................
                 PASSION OR INDUSTRY                TIME, YEAR, AGE, GRADE

when I...............................................................................................................................
               KEY EXPERIENCE

From there it grew. I started ...............................................................................................
                  NEW ACTIONS (Groups, Books, Subscriptions, Practice, etc.)

...............................................................................................................................

Today my passion is like never before. I continue to .......................................................
                       FORMS OF PRACTICE

...............................................................................................................................

in addition to ....................................................................................................................

I created this blog to start a conversation, and to learn from, and connect with those who share my passion. The top 3 resources that have supported me on my journey include:

1. ...................................................................................................................................

2. ...................................................................................................................................

3. ...................................................................................................................................

Please share any resources that have helped influence your passion by commenting below.

Until next time,

**PROBLEM BLOG**

**Key Questions:**
- What is the biggest problem in your industry today?
- What are your ideas on how it can be solved?
- What new innovations do you see potentially solving this problem? Which ones won't be effective and why?

**Entry Title: The Biggest Problem For [YOUR TARGET INDUSTRY] Today**

The ................................................... is evolving quickly as is the rest of the world.
                          INDUSTRY

I remember when..............................................................................................................
                          MEMORY ABOUT THE INDUSTRY 5-10 YEARS AGO

Since then, there have been three major trends that I've observed, and I think we need to take them into consideration because they will likely change the industry forever.

1. ............................................................................................................................

............................................................................................................................

2. ............................................................................................................................

............................................................................................................................

3. ............................................................................................................................

............................................................................................................................

The convergence of these three trends could result in........................................................

............................................................................................................................

............................................................................................................................

Thus a great threat or opportunity (depending on how you look at it) is upon us. If you have any interesting thoughts, statistics, or opinions, feel free to leave them in the comments section below.

Thanks in advance,

**INDUSTRY NEWS BLOG**

**Key Questions:**
- What recent trends do you see in your industry? Who is impacted most by them? How do the trends affect decision making?
- If you could envision your industry 10 years from now, what would it look like?
- What are some of your assumptions about the future of your industry?

**Entry Title: Response To [AUTHOR]'s Ideas On [SUBJECT]**

I recently read ............................................................ article (book or blog) titled
AUTHOR

............................................................................................................................
TITLE

His/her main point can be captured in the quote, "............................................................

............................................................................................................................

............................................................................................................................"

I totally dis/agree and here's why:

First and foremost, ..........................................................................................................

............................................................................................................................

On top of that,................................................................................................................

............................................................................................................................

Finally, ...........................................................................................................................

............................................................................................................................

In my opinion, our industry undervalues (or overvalues)......................................................

............................................................................................................................

Until we put the appropriate value on...............................................................................
SUBJECT OF DEBATE

we won't realize our true potential to ...............................................................................
PURPOSE OF INDUSTRY

# 2.15 HOW TO EDIT ALL OF YOUR COPY FOR CONSISTENCY & GRAMMAR

The worst thing that can happen with any job application is to mention how "detail-oriented" you are in your cover letter but then have all kinds of grammatical errors within the one-page document. That creates an inconsistency between who you say you are and what the potential employer is actually observing in the moment. Even something that small makes them ask themselves: "About what other things may he (or she) not be fully honest?" Grammatical errors fog the lens through which potential employers see you, and you want them to see you clearly for who you truly are so they can make the best decision for themselves and you.

Grammar is just one form of inconsistency. Other common inconsistencies include:
• Having the wrong company name or position on your cover letter suggesting that you are using a template instead of customizing each application.
• Incongruence between your printed and online brand (e.g., your online brand stating your passion for marketing, but your cover letter and résumé projecting finance).
• Jobs or references on your cover letter that don't appear on your résumé
• Language or claims on your cover letter, bio, or blogs that aren't supported by your Résumé 1.0 or Résumé 2.0.
• Unexplained gaps in the chronology of your résumé.

The best way to catch errors in spelling, grammar, and consistency is to have three sets of fresh eyes look at all of your D.R.E.A.M. catchers (Résumé 1.0, Résumé 2.0, blog, website, etc.) from the perspective of an HR manager to see if they complement or contradict one another. You can reach out to career advisors, friends who love writing, and mentors. Keep in mind that everyone isn't a professional editor, but their varied experiences and perspective will cause them to catch different things and come up with different questions that you have to reconcile once you receive all of their feedback.

In this section, you simply have to gather all of your D.R.E.A.M. catchers and find people who are willing to support you in making sure your professional story is consistent and of quality. All of the documents they need to provide you adequate feedback are on the following pages. Print out three sets along with three sets of your D.R.E.A.M. catchers and give them an adequate timeline to do a thorough reading of your materials.

## PEER EDITING KIT

**Student's Name:**...................................................................................................

**Editor's Name:**.....................................................................................................

**Due Date:**................................... **Phone Number:**........................................................

Thank you for agreeing to edit and audit my personal brand. The purpose of this activity is to develop my personal and professional brand and ensure quality and consistency.

**Steps for each document:**
1. Please read each document out loud to yourself.
2. Circle all spelling errors and areas of confusion.
3. Mark YES (Y) or NO (N) in the boxes for each question below.

**Business Card**

| Y | N | |
|---|---|---|
| | | Are there any spelling errors? Please circle them. |
| | | Are there any confusing uses of language? Please circle them. |
| | | Does the superhero name intrigue you and make you want to know more? |
| | | Does the contact information match the information on the résumé? |

**Additional thoughts, feedback, or comments:**

...................................................................................................

...................................................................................................

...................................................................................................

...................................................................................................

...................................................................................................

...................................................................................................

...................................................................................................

...................................................................................................

...................................................................................................

**RÉSUMÉ 1.0**

| Y | N | |
|---|---|---|
| | | Are there any spelling errors? Please circle them. |
| | | Are there any confusing uses of language? Please circle them. |
| | | Is the layout clean and clear? |
| | | Does each bullet point communicate how the individual moved something (a number, initiative, etc.) from some point A to some point B |
| | | Are there any gaps in the dates on the résumé? |
| | | Does the name and contact information on the résumé match what you see on the business card? |
| | | Do the résumé bullet points read like they were copied from a job description instead of reading like results created by the individual? |

**Additional thoughts, feedback, or comments:**

...............................................................................................................................

...............................................................................................................................

...............................................................................................................................

...............................................................................................................................

...............................................................................................................................

...............................................................................................................................

...............................................................................................................................

...............................................................................................................................

...............................................................................................................................

...............................................................................................................................

...............................................................................................................................

**RÉSUMÉ 2.0**

| Y | N | |
|---|---|---|
| | | Are there any spelling errors? Please circle them. |
| | | Are there any confusing uses of language? Please circle them. |
| | | Is the layout clean and clear? |
| | | Does each slide have a clear title and purpose? |
| | | Do the images complement the text? |

**Additional thoughts, feedback, or comments:**

............................................................................................................................

............................................................................................................................

............................................................................................................................

............................................................................................................................

............................................................................................................................

............................................................................................................................

............................................................................................................................

............................................................................................................................

............................................................................................................................

............................................................................................................................

............................................................................................................................

............................................................................................................................

............................................................................................................................

............................................................................................................................

............................................................................................................................

**THREE BLOG ENTRIES**

| Y | N | |
|---|---|---|
| | | Are there any spelling errors? Please circle them. |
| | | Are there any confusing uses of language? Please circle them. |
| | | Does the blog entry about a PROBLEM convey that the individual has deep INSIGHTS about the industry? |
| | | Does the blog entry about a PASSION convey that the individual has deep COMMITMENT to the industry? |
| | | Does the blog entry about the INDUSTRY convey that the individual has a clear VISION about the industry? |
| | | Does the blog entry about the PUBLICATION convey that the individual has INNOVATIVE THOUGHTS about the industry? |

**Additional thoughts, feedback, or comments:**

..................................................................................................................................

..................................................................................................................................

..................................................................................................................................

..................................................................................................................................

..................................................................................................................................

..................................................................................................................................

..................................................................................................................................

..................................................................................................................................

..................................................................................................................................

..................................................................................................................................

..................................................................................................................................

..................................................................................................................................

## WEBSITE OR BLOG HOMEPAGE

| Y | N | |
|---|---|---|
| | | Are there any spelling errors? Please circle them. |
| | | Are there any confusing uses of language? Please circle them. |
| | | Does the individual's 30 second pitch capture you? |
| | | Does the picture in the header look professional? |
| | | Does the "More About Me" section give you insight into the individuals's personality and life outside of work? |
| | | Is the Résumé 1.0 "Google Doc" displaying properly? |
| | | Is the Résumé 2.0 "slideshow" displaying properly and working? |
| | | Does the "download résumé" link work? |

**Additional thoughts, feedback, or comments:**

..................................................................................................................

..................................................................................................................

..................................................................................................................

..................................................................................................................

..................................................................................................................

..................................................................................................................

..................................................................................................................

..................................................................................................................

..................................................................................................................

..................................................................................................................

..................................................................................................................

# IMMEDIATELY RETURN THESE FORMS TO THE PERSON WHO GAVE THEM TO YOU.

# 2.16 HOW TO MAXIMIZE YOUR LINKEDIN & FACEBOOK PROFILES & EXPAND YOUR NETWORKS

LinkedIn.com and Facebook.com are powerful professional tools even if that hasn't been their primary use for you up until this point. Social media has become integrated into the hiring process on the employer side and the employee side. Employers use social media to learn more about potential employees in the same way they use references. Employees use them to get inside information about the employers by finding friends who already work for those employers.

As an employee, here are some statistics that you should know about hiring managers and social media:
• Nearly one in two hiring managers uses social media to recruit or screen candidates for jobs today
• More than a third of hiring managers (35 percent) immediately screen out candidates based on what they find on candidates' social networking profiles.

LinkedIn.com is powerful because it allows you to find your friends based on industry and company. You may have friends or acquaintances who already work where you are applying to work, and they can provide vital information as well as push your résumé to the top of the pile. In addition to that, LinkedIn lets you store your recommendations from other professionals online so that when someone finds you, they can see the recommendations and learn more about who it's coming from. Finally, LinkedIn.com can serve as an online version of your résumé if you complete your profile thoroughly. LinkedIn.com works best when your network is big, so start inviting people using the e-mail contacts function immediately.

While Facebook.com is primarily social, it has its professional benefits as well. You can also find your friends by company and city. More so than anything though, your Facebook.com profile should be clean and semi-professional, meaning that you have a nice profile picture and monitor what you put on your page as well as what other people type on your page, and the pictures they tag you in. You can also adjust what visitors see by setting appropriate privacy settings.

It would be terrible to lose a job opportunity for which you are a perfect fit just because of a silly profile picture that you put up just for fun. That doesn't have to be the case. Even if you have a great website, you should also have a great presence in social media as well.

## LINKEDIN.COM

**Directions:** Complete the checklist of items below to enhance your LinkedIn.com presence and network.

## EDITING YOUR LINKEDIN.COM PROFILE

### Overall
❏ Complete the profile as thoroughly as possible

### Basic Info
❏ When editing your profile, put your superhero name for your "Professional Headline"
❏ Upload your professional photo

### Current & Past Employment
❏ Add your last three most significant positions and copy and paste the bullet-points from your résumé into the description.
❏ If the company you worked for is not a Fortune .500 company, add one or two sentences about it at the top of your description
❏ If you've been promoted within the same organization, add those positions separately (to show your growth).

### Recommendations
❏ Request recommendations for specific positions (ideally one to two per position). Don't ask randomly. Call the person first. Tell him or her than an e-mail from LinkedIn is coming and offer to recommend that person in return.

### Additional Information
❏ For websites put www.yourname.com as your website and add www.yourname.com/blog as your blog.
❏ Add all of your passions to the interest section.
❏ Add all of your organizational affiliations (e.g., young professional group, church, fraternity, sorority, etc.).

### Personal Information
❏ Add only your phone number (preferably a Google Voice number that forwards to your real cell phone).

### Public Profile
❏ Edit it to be www.linkedin.com/in/yourname.

### Applications
❏ Link your résumé 2.0 from Slideshare.net.

## EXPANDING YOUR LINKEDIN.COM NETWORK

### ADDING CONTACTS

#### Import from E-mail
1. Go to https://www.linkedin.com/fetch/importAndInvite.
2. Enter the e-mail address from which you want to import contacts from.
3. Enter your password.
4. Select only people with the [IN] symbol next to their names. It may take a while to go through everyone, but it will help your research later.

#### Import Colleagues
1. Go to http://www.linkedin.com/reconnect?displayCategories=&trk=tab_cols.
2. Select only the names of colleagues with whom you have worked on projects or at least with whom you have had lunch with.

#### Import Classmates
1. Go to http://www.linkedin.com/edurec?display=&trk=tab_clas.
2. Select only classmates you would run after to talk to in an airport.

#### People You May Know
1. Go to http://www.linkedin.com/pymk-results?full=.
2. Select only people who you actually know.

#### Groups
1. Go to http://www.linkedin.com/groupsDirectory.
2. Find any groups or organizations with which you may be affiliated with (e.g., schools, fraternities, sororities, programs, etc.).

#### Evaluating Your Social Capital
1. Go to http://www.linkedin.com/connections?trk=hb_tab_cnts.
2. Click the "colleagues" tag to see current and old colleagues.
3. Click the "classmates" tag to see current and old classmates.
4. Click "Companies" and you will see the top 10 companies where you have the most contacts at.
5. Click "Location" and you will see the top 10 cities/regions where you have the most contacts in.
6. Click "Industries" and you will see the top 10 industries that where have the most contacts in.
7. For 4, 5, & 6, to send a message, select all or select the individuals in the second column, and then click "Send Message" in the third column.

## FACEBOOK.COM

**Directions:** Complete the checklist of items below to enhance your Facebook.com presence and network.

### EDITING YOUR FACEBOOK.COM PROFILE

#### Overall
❐ Complete the profile with the eye of an HR representative without losing who you are.

#### About Me
1. Condense your 30-second pitch to 15 seconds and paste it in the area under your profile picture.
2. In the "Bio" section of your profile, either put www.yourname.com or copy the "More About Me" section from www.yourname.com.
3. In the "Favorite Quotations" section, add a quote from someone you respect in your industry. For instance, I might put something like:

   *"A real decision is measured by the fact that you've taken a new action. If there's no action, you haven't truly decided."* - Tony Robbins

#### Photos
1. Roll over your profile photo in the upper right hand corner, click "Change picture," and upload your professional picture.
2. Upload other professional profile pictures to balance out your personal ones.
3. Click on your profile photo and save the ones to your desktop that you want to keep and then delete any "crazy" pictures.
4. Skim through all of your photos to make sure there aren't any compromising photos there. Make sure to skim the photos you were tagged in and untag yourself if necessary.

#### Work & Education
1. Replicate what you did on LinkedIn.
2. Add your "concentrations." It will help you with search later.

#### Books
1. Add to your favorite books list some of the books you've read that are related to the industry.

#### Contact Information
1. Add your firstname@yourname.com to your e-mail address.
2. Add your Google Voice number to your profile.
3. Add www.yourname.com as your websites.

#### Importing Your Blog
1. Go to http://www.facebook.com/editnotes.php?import.
2. Enter www.julliengordon.weebly.com/1/feed.

**Getting Your Custom URL**
1.  Go to http://www.facebook.com/username.
2.  Change your Facebook profile address to www.facebook.com/yourname
(i.e. www.facebook.com/jullien or www.facebook.com/julliengordon).

**Finding Friends By City & Company**
1. Go to your profile.
2. Click on "Friends" under your profile picture.
3. At the top of the page, click on the menu that says "Search by Name" and go down to
    "Search by Workplace" or "Search by City."
4. Type in the workplace or city in which you are considering working in.

**EXPANDING YOUR FACEBOOK.COM NETWORK**

**ADDING CONTACTS**

**Import from E-mail**
1. Go to http://www.facebook.com/find-friends/?ref=sb.
2. Enter the e-mail address you want to import contacts from.
3. Enter your password.
4. You will be befriended to everyone you select.

**Suggested Friends**
1.  Go to http://www.facebook.com/find-friends/?expand=pymk&ref=hpb.
2.  Click "Add as friend" on people you recognize.

1. CREATE YOUR
   D.R.E.A.M. LIFE

2. ATTRACT YOUR
   D.R.E.A.M. CAREER

3. **BUILD YOUR
   D.R.E.A.M. TEAM**

4. LAND YOUR
   D.R.E.A.M. JOB

# 3.1 HOW TO BUILD YOUR SOCIAL CAPITAL IN 30 DAYS

Although you're probably comfortable searching for jobs at your computer, that strategy doesn't yield the best results; your network will be more important than the Internet. According to the Impact Group 2010 report on career explorers, networking was the most effective method for landing a job (at a 34 percent success rate), and applying online was second (26 percent). Among networking approaches, referrals from within the organization (18 percent) and outside the organization (9 percent) are the most successful ways to land the opportunity. They also found that 26.7 percent of external hires made by organizations came from referrals, making it the number one external source of hiring for the participating firms.

It's one thing to find your D.R.E.A.M. job posting, but it's just as important to know the people who are making decisions about who gets that position. Therefore, your job search is a search for the right people, more so than the right positions or postings. So, the greater your social capital—who you know and who knows you—the greater your ability to find the right people and get them to move on your behalf.

Most students try to endure the career discovery process alone, but finding a career isn't the same as finding a job during high school or college when you could walk into a restaurant on your own and submit an application. The more people who are searching with you, the better. But the secret to a successful career search isn't just enrolling your friends who think like you and know the same people as you. The secret is to tap into **decentralized networks**.

## TYPES OF NETWORKS

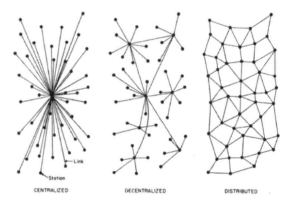

CENTRALIZED          DECENTRALIZED          DISTRIBUTED

These networks are where mentors, career advisors, professors, parents, parents' friends, aunts, uncles, guest speakers, and other professionals come in. Together they make up your **personal board of directors**. You are tapping into a **distributed network** in which very few contacts in the cell phone of the other person match the contacts in your phone. A distributed network is when someone you know personally has the contact information of someone you need to know. That someone can connect you in person, via phone, e-mail, LinkedIn, or Facebook. In a distributed network, someone you would like to meet is usually within three degrees of separation. In a **centralized network**, you are the hub or connector. This is great, but it is harder to sustain this many relationships at a time. Rather than managing a centralized network, it would be easier to maintain a few relationships with connectors who have centralized networks themselves.

Therefore, you want to make sure you network up, down, across, and out to maximize your social capital.

**Networking Up:** Networking up involves meeting people who are older than you or have more access to what you want such as mentors, professors, parents, old bosses, aunts, uncles, and alumni. Up is the most powerful direction to network because these people can get you through the doors you're knocking on.

**Networking Down:** Networking down involves maintaining relationships with mentees, younger siblings, and organizations that helped you succeed. They are invested in your success and may have connections to people you need to know.

**Networking Across:**
Networking across involves your peers, **30 Day Do It Group (See Module 3.5),** classmates, and anyone else who is at a similar stage as you. Industry colleagues usually don't count because it may not be in your best interest to tell a colleague you are looking elsewhere.

**Networking Out:** Networking out involves intentionally seeking to meet people outside of your existing networks by going to network events and

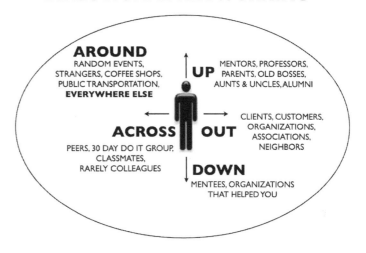

**DIRECTIONAL NETWORKING**

conferences where new people who share your passion may be. If you're already in a company, it means building relationships with clients, customers, organizations, and associations. In many cases, companies that do business together "steal" valuable players from each other.

**Networking Around:** Networking around involves seeing every moment as a networking opportunity. It means going to random events, talking to strangers at the coffee shop, at the grocery store, on public transportation, or an airplane. You never know who you sitting or standing next to and what you can do for them and vice versa.

Effective networking isn't about the quantity of people you know—it's about the quality of people and the quality of their networks. It's also about being open to the fact that anyone can be a great resource if you're open to building the relationship by contributing to his or her life in any way you can by leveraging your capital to be helpful.

**Directions:** Identify networking events you want to go to and track your results from each event.

## EVENT SCHEDULER

| NAME/EVENT | DATE & TIME | LOCATION |
|---|---|---|
| Mark Addington of ACME INC | 7/7 @ 12pm | Starbucks on 51st |
| | | |
| | | |
| | | |
| | | |
| | | |
| | | |
| | | |
| | | |
| | | |
| | | |
| | | |
| | | |
| | | |
| | | |
| | | |

## EVENT SCHEDULER

| RESULTS | FOLLOW UP E-MAILS |
|---|---|
| Passing my résumé on internally & to industry friends. | sent |
| | |
| | |
| | |
| | |
| | |
| | |
| | |
| | |
| | |
| | |
| | |
| | |
| | |
| | |

## PERSONAL BOARD OF DIRECTORS

**Directions:** Network with 6 people in each direction and schedule meetings using the e-mail template provided to create your personal board of directors.

**30 DAY DO IT GROUP:** Friends who came to your first 30 Day Do It Group meeting.

1........................................................ 4........................................................

2........................................................ 5........................................................

3........................................................ 6........................................................

**NETWORK UP:** Mentors, Professors, Family, Family Friends, and Old Bosses.

7........................................................ 10........................................................

8........................................................ 11........................................................

9........................................................ 12........................................................

**NETWORK ACROSS:** Friends, Old Classmates, Neighbors, Alumni Events.

13........................................................ 16........................................................

14........................................................ 17........................................................

15........................................................ 18........................................................

**NETWORK OUT:** Client's companies, Organizations that helped you, Associations to which you belong, Honors Societies, Organizations for which you've volunteered.

19........................................................ 22........................................................

20........................................................ 23........................................................

21........................................................ 24........................................................

**NETWORK AROUND:** Meetup.com, Networking events, Strangers, Everywhere.

25........................................................ 28........................................................

26........................................................ 29........................................................

27........................................................ 30........................................................

## INVITATION E-MAIL TEMPLATE

Hi ........................................................,

It's always good seeing you at ...................................................................
EVENT, PLACE, OR ORGANIZATION

I admire your .............................................................................................
AFFIRMATION

and that's exactly the reason I'm reaching out to you.

I'm seeking to accelerate my career and I need some of your.....................................
SKILL YOU AFFIRMED

I'm currently a ............................................. at ........................................,
CURRENT POSITION                              CURRENT COLLEGE/COMPANY

but I would like to transition into ...............................................................
D.R.E.A.M. JOB OR INDUSTRY

Considering my passion for ...........................................................................
PASSION, SKILL, AND/OR SUBJECT

I was hoping I could have 15 minutes of your time for a call, quick coffee, or even lunch (whatever works best for you).

You seem to love your work and that inspires me. I just want to know if you know of any opportunities that may fit me, have any contacts in the industry, or have general strategies that may help me along my career path.

I've attached my résumé, but you can also view it online at ...........................................
www.yourname.com

Let me know if you have the time.

Thanks in advance,

...................................................
YOUR NAME

# HOW TO LEAVE WITH REAL RELATIONSHIPS & FOLLOW UP USING T.E.C.H.

To get a job, to find a date, or to get new clients are some common answers for why people go to networking events, but the original intention of networking events was to meet people you need to know that you don't already know. There are a few major issues with networking events that prevent them from being effective, and they are that most people:

1. Go to networking events to gain rather than to give.
2. Leave networking events with stacks of business cards and no real relationships.
3. Try to be who they aren't at networking events, but most people actually crave authenticity.

These issues lead to shallow relationships and are ultimately a waste of time for everyone. Through **Network Visioning** you can transform the way people experience you and the way you experience them by following these simple rules:

1. Seek to be a contribution first.
2. Make your goal a relationship (not a card).
3. Project that the real you is amazing, and so is the real me.

The law of reciprocity suggests that when you give first, your likelihood of receiving increases. You can try it with a business card. If getting a business card is your goal, start by giving yours first. The exchange of business cards is like a ritual, and it's rare that only one person gives.

However, the goal of networking is not just business cards—it's to form a real relationship. Networking should be considered the start of a long-term relationship rather than a quick moment that two people meet. Perhaps the two people don't discover any business opportunities in their first conversation, but over time other ways for them to help each other will emerge, if they stay in touch.

Finally, the coolest people at networking events are the people with an interesting story. Although networking tends to begin with a facade of status and success, people really want to get to know you for who you are and also be known for who they are. If you cultivate interest, it's important to follow up using the **Texting, E-Mail, Call, and Host (T.E.C.H.)** in a sequence so that a good relationship doesn't fall through the cracks.

In this section, you will learn the five steps to network visioning so that you get the results you want in the moment and, most importantly, afterward.

After the event, the next step is following up. All business card exchanges are well intentioned, but follow-up is where relationships get dropped. The key to following up is finding what technological language the person you met speaks so that you can communicate with them the way they like to communicate. Within two weeks, here is how you can use T.E.C.H. (Text/Tweet, E-mail, Call, & Host) to build new relationships.

## TEXT or TWEET

The morning after you meet, you should send a quick text message (if you got someone's cell phone number or tweet) about how awesome he or she is (if you got their Twitter handle). Below are some examples of a text and a tweet.

*TEXT:*
*Hi Alex. It's Jullien. Great meeting you at last night's event. Expect an e-mail by Thursday.*

*TWEET:*
*Graduating soon? Check out @PurposeFinder's amazing videos at* http:// www.julliengordon.com. *Met last night. Awesome!*

## E-MAIL

Within 24-48 hours after the text message, you should deliver on the e-mail you proposed in the text message. The e-mail should read as follows:

*SUBJECT:  Hi Alex. It's Jullien from Tuesday's Speed Networking Event.*

*BODY: Hi Alex,*

*Thanks for the good conversation and laughs last night. I'm glad we met.*

## 1. Recommendations

*Check out the recommendations we discussed when you get a chance.*

*Daniel Pink's Drive 2.0:* http://www.amazon.com/Drive
*The HR Organization:* http://www.hrorg.org

## 2. www.julliengordon.com

*My résumé 1.0, résumé 2.0, Facebook, LinkedIn, Twitter, and other contact information can all be found here. Please forward it on to anyone you think might be interested.*

## 3. 30 Day Do It Group

If you're interested, my next 30 Day Do It Group is on June 6, 2010, at 7pm at 1342 Longley Ave, Brooklyn, NY. I hope you can make it. If not this month, then sometime in the near future.

Take care,

# FOLLOWING UP WITH T.E.C.H.

| MON | TUES | WED | THUR | FRI | SAT | SUN |
|---|---|---|---|---|---|---|
| | | | | | | |
| | | | | | | |
| | | **1. TEXT** TOMORROW MORNING | | **2. EMAIL** 24-48 HOURS AFTER THE TEXT | | |
| | | **3. CALL** ONE WEEK LATER (ONLY IF URGENT) | | **4. HOST** INVITATION ONE WEEK BEFORE YOUR EVENT | | |
| | | | | | | |

**YOUR EVENT:** GALA, 30 DAY DO IT, ETC

# NETWORK VISIONING

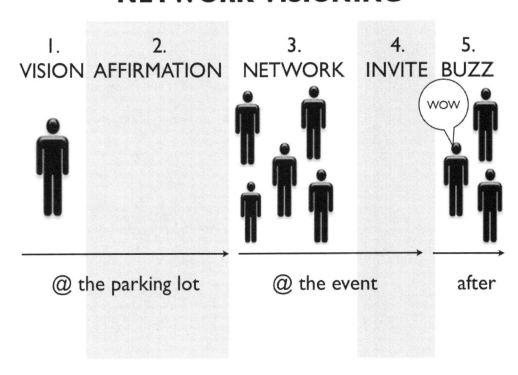

1. VISION  2. AFFIRMATION  3. NETWORK  4. INVITE  5. BUZZ

WOW

@ the parking lot    @ the event    after

## CALL

If there is no response after a week and they made a commitment that you need them to deliver on, you should give your new acquaintance a quick call. If that person doesn't pick up, you can use the voice-mail template below:

*VOICE-MAIL:*
*Hi Alex. It's Jullien Gordon. We met briefly at the networking event last Tuesday. I'm just following up to make sure you got my e-mail with the information I promised, and to see if you had ten to fifteen minutes to give me some industry insight and career advice. My number is (646) 875-8000. Again that's (646) 875-8000. Thanks in advance.*

## HOST

When technology fails to sustain the relationship, go back to the old way and invite new acquaintances to an event you're hosting or choose another event from which you think those persons would gain extreme value. Instead of beginning with a 1-on-1 engagement like a lunch, make it easier on everyone and invite them to a place where lots of awesome people will be so they can have a great time without you being always by their side. Send them an e-mail one week before an event and make the invitation sound exclusive.

*SUBJECT: Hi Alex. Join Me And A Group Of Go-Getters On Friday*

*BODY: Hi Alex,*

*I hope all is well. I want to invite you as one of my two guests to a forum of thirty amazing entrepreneurs, techies, and geeks.*

*This "30 Day Do It" group is happening on June 6, 2010, at 7 p.m. at 1342 Longley Ave, New York, NY. I hope you can make it. If not this month, then sometime in the near future.*

*Take care,*

If you follow this follow-up format, you will have made a concerted effort to build a lasting relationship with someone. If the person doesn't respond to any of your invitations, don't take it personally and focus your energy on building other new relationships.

## 1. HOW DO YOU WANT PEOPLE TO SPEAK ABOUT YOU AFTER THE EVENT?

**Directions:** Imagine that the professional you met at last night's networking event just arrived at his or her office the next morning and is pulling out your business card to give to a colleague. Use the template below to envision what you would want that person to say about you.

I recently met a wo/man by the name of.................................................................................
FULL NAME

She calls her/himself the .................................................................................................
SUPERHERO NAME

S/he says s/he has a unique ability to ....................................................................................

.................................................................................................................................
SUPER POWER

We talked for about .......... minutes about ...........................................................................

.................................................................................................................................
TOPICS OF CONVERSATION (INDUSTRY, PASSIONS, PROBLEMS, ETC.)

I thought what s/he had to say was...........................................................................................
FEELING ABOUT YOUR INSIGHTS AND EXPERTISE

Here's her/his card. I think you should really check out her/his website and ....................

.................................................................................................................................
ACTION YOU WANT THAT PERSON TO RECOMMEND THEIR FRIEND TAKES

NOTE: This also accounts for step five in the network visioning process.

## 2. WHAT HAPPENS FOR PEOPLE'S LIVES WHEN I'M AROUND?

### PARKING LOT AFFIRMATION
*I am independent AND available. I am about giving (not getting), passion (not profession), listening (not talking), and being a contribution (not business cards).*

**Directions:** Answer the question "Who do you have to BE when you enter this room to have someone talk about you positively to someone else?"

**Example:** I am the PurposeFinder. When I am present, people:
**1.** Start thinking about their purpose more and see what's possible for their own lives.
**2.** Feel more motivated to accomplish their goals.
**3.** Hear their inner voice a lot clearer.


I am a/the ............................................................!
              SUPERHERO NAME


When I am present, people (see/feel/hear/taste/smell/sense/etc.):


1....................................................................................................................................
              WHAT HAPPENS FOR PEOPLE'S LIVES WHEN YOU ARE AROUND


.........................................................................................................................................


2....................................................................................................................................
              WHAT HAPPENS FOR PEOPLE'S LIVES WHEN YOU ARE AROUND


.........................................................................................................................................


3....................................................................................................................................
              WHAT HAPPENS FOR PEOPLE'S LIVES WHEN YOU ARE AROUND


.........................................................................................................................................

## 3. WHAT WOULD I EXPECT MYSELF TO DO?

**Directions:** Answer the question " What do you have to DO when you enter this room to have someone talk about you positively to someone else?"

**Example:** As a PurposeFinder, I would:
1. Ask people who look lost what they're looking for and point them in the right direction.
2. Introduce people with similar purposes.
3. Ask "So what are you passionate about?" instead of "So, what do you do?"
4. Guide people to resources that will help them on their journey.

**WHAT WOULD A** ...................................................... **DO?**
SUPERHERO NAME

1.......................................................................................................................

.......................................................................................................................

2.......................................................................................................................

.......................................................................................................................

3.......................................................................................................................

.......................................................................................................................

4.......................................................................................................................

.......................................................................................................................

5.......................................................................................................................

.......................................................................................................................

## 4. MY INVITATION TO GO DEEPER

**Directions:** Complete the "Invitation To Go Deeper" template below and use it during the exchange of business cards.

I really enjoyed our conversation.

Now I know that when most people exchange business cards, 90 percent of the time it means that they will not have the opportunity to talk again, but if you're open to it, I would like to invite you to a monthly group I host of some pretty amazing people.

It's called a 30 Day Do It Group.

Basically, every 30 days, a group of highly ......................................................................
TWO ADJECTIVES (E.G., MOTIVATED OR INTELLIGENT)

..................................................................................................................................
DESCRIPTOR OF GROUP MEMBERS (E.G., GEEKS, YOUNG PROFESSIONALS, ENTREPRENEURS)

get together and set one goal for the month. It's called your new month resolution.

But when you set that goal, you also create a cost for not achieving it. For instance, I bet everyone that I would pay them $40 each if I don't accomplish my goal this month.

The higher the cost you set, the greater the chance that you'll complete your goal.

You can use it for any type of goal—personal, professional, family, physical, financial.

Our next meeting is on .............................................. in ..........................................
                DAY, DATE, & TIME                            CITY/LOCATION

I'll include the details in my follow up e-mail.

Seriously, if there is anything in your life that isn't where you want it be, this is the way to move it. On top of that you'll meet more great people.

What's a goal or project you have in mind that you've been stuck or moving slow on?

# 3.3 HOW TO SOUND LIKE AN EXPERT AT ANY NETWORKING EVENT

There are a few ways to get people's attention while networking to ensure that you get remembered. One way is to use one's personal capital and tell an interesting personal story. Another common way is to leverage one's social capital and name drop about who you know. When it's inauthentic and irrelevant, name dropping is a turn off. The most obnoxious way is to use one's financial capital and buy things in the moment or talk about the things one recently bought.

The most appropriate form of capital to display during networking is your intellectual capital. Intellectual capital is the easiest to convey when networking because the currency is words of wisdom and insight. Social capital's currency is real relationships, which is a given since you're at the same event. Personal capital's currency is self-awareness, which will come across, but it may be too personal. Financial capital's currency is money, and it is irrelevant in any initial meeting.

In order for your intellectual capital to come through, you must do some pre-work, and that pre-work involves reading and research. No matter what industry you are targeting, it is always helpful when networking to be aware of the hot topics, the go-to book, the latest related TED.com Talk, and a company or person that is shaking up the industry.

| Example Industries | Technology | Education |
|---|---|---|
| Top Article or Blog | Apple killing SMS | Live & Learn (New Yorker) |
| Top Book or Movie | The Innovator's Dilemma | Waiting on Superman |
| Top TED.com Talk | Eli Pariser "Filter Bubbles" | Sir Ken Robinson |
| Top Company or Person | Groupon.com | KhanAcademy.org |

Whether you bring it up in a conversation or someone else does, having an opinion or perspective will show your competence, diligence, awareness, and critical thinking skills. The alternative is to be perceived as incompetent, lazy, unaware, and uninteresting.

In this section are some ways you can find out what's going on in your industry before a networking opportunity, and templates you can use to start or contribute to conversations that develop at an event.

### Top Article
1. Go to http://news.google.com.
2. In the search box, type in your industry (e.g., banking, non-profit, marketing).
3. Choose an interesting article and click on the link.
4. Read it and then use the template below to formulate an interesting opinion for conversation.
5. Also read the comments. They have interesting thoughts and opinions.

### Top Blog
1. Go to http://alltop.com.
2. In the search box, type in your industry (e.g., banking, non-profit, marketing).
3. Click on the result that best matches your search term.
4. Choose one of the most popular stories and click on the link.
5. Also read the comments. They have interesting thoughts and opinions.

### Top Book
1. Go to http://www.amazon.com.
2. Select the "Books" category.
3. In the search box, type in your industry (e.g., banking, non-profit, marketing).
4. Under "New Releases" in the upper left-hand corner, select "Last 90 Days".
5. Copy the book title.
6. Go to http://www.google.com.
7. Paste the book title into the search box and click search.
8. Find and read an article about the book's release.
9. Use the template below to formulate an interesting opinion for conversation.
10. If possible, order the book and read it.

### Top TED.com Talk
1. Go to http://www.ted.com.
2. In the search box, type in your industry (e.g., banking, non-profit, marketing).
3. Choose one of the videos that interests you most.
4. Watch the 18 minute video and then use the template below to formulate an interesting opinion for conversation.

### Top Company or Person
1. Go to http://news.google.com.
2. In the search box, type in a company or person's name you want to research.
3. Choose an interesting article and click on the link.
4. Read it and then use the template below to formulate an interesting opinion for conversation.
5. Also read the comments. They have interesting thoughts and opinions.

**Directions:** Use the templates below to formulate an interesting opinion for each conversation starter.

## TOP ARTICLE OR BLOG

................................................................ had a great article I think you should check out
    THE BLOG, MAGAZINE, OR PAPER NAME

on ........................................................ The writer's main argument in the article was
    PASSION, PROBLEM, OR INDUSTRY

................................................................................................................................

................................................................................................................................

I really thought that his or her point about ........................................................................

was very interesting because..............................................................................................

................................................................................................................................

Based on your experience, what do you think about the argument?

## TOP BOOK

Have you read.............................................................. by ................................................
               BOOK TITLE                       AUTHOR

It's about ........................................................................ The main premise is
        PASSION, PROBLEM, OR INDUSTRY

................................................................................................................................

................................................................................................................................

................................................................................................................................

I really thought that the point about .................................................................................

was very interesting because..............................................................................................

................................................................................................................................

What do you think about the premise?

## TOP TED.COM TALK

................................................................ gave a great talk at TED I think you should see
<br>PRESENTER'S NAME

on ................................................................ The main point during the talk was
<br>PASSION, PROBLEM, OR INDUSTRY

................................................................................................................................

................................................................................................................................

................................................................................................................................

I really thought that the point about ................................................................................

was very interesting because................................................................................

................................................................................................................................

What do you think about................................................................................?
<br>TED TALK TOPIC

## TOP COMPANY OR PERSON

Have you heard of..........................................................? I hear that he (or she) is doing
<br>COMPANY OR PERSON NAME

some pretty awesome work regarding................................................................
<br>PASSION, PROBLEM, OR INDUSTRY

I recently read that................................................................................

................................................................................................................................

................................................................................................................................

................................................................................................................................

How do you think that kind of innovation could affect the marketplace?

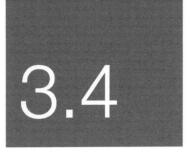

# 3.4 HOW TO EXECUTE A POWERFUL 30-MINUTE GET-LINKED-IN CONVERSATION

If you are lost and looking for direction, the only way others can help you is if you tell them where you are and where you are trying to go. Otherwise, no matter whose ear you have, and how much they want to help you, they can't.

Whether your next interaction with those you meet at a networking event is via phone or in person, you can use the **Get-Linked-In Conversation** to prepare for the engagement so that you maximize both your time, and the **Call Map** so that they feel useful to you by leaving you with a sense of direction.

The goal of a follow-up call or meeting is two-fold:

1. To be a contribution to their life and/or work
2. To access capital and resources—people, organizations, tools, opportunities, and ideas—that you didn't know about or didn't have access to before.

You should seek to give first and then receive. You can start by giving:
• Information (be vulnerable and valuable).
• Ideas (tools, recommendations).
• Time (volunteer, service)

When it's your turn to receive, you should provide them with the answers to the following questions and then prepare to listen to the wisdom and insights they have based on their experiences. To prepare for your next engagement, answer these questions:

1. Why did you call them?
2. Why are you on this journey?
3. Where are you on your journey?
4. Where are you trying to go?
5. What tools do you have with you?
6. What are your biggest challenges?

Use the Call Map and templates in this section to help you prepare for your next engagement with new professional relationships.

## CALL MAP

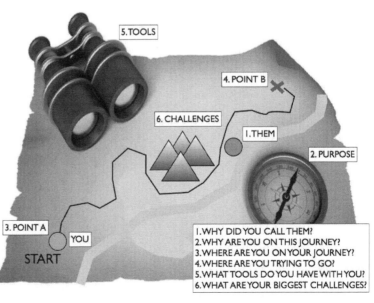

5. TOOLS

4. POINT B

6. CHALLENGES

1. THEM

2. PURPOSE

3. POINT A

YOU

START

1. WHY DID YOU CALL THEM?
2. WHY ARE YOU ON THIS JOURNEY?
3. WHERE ARE YOU ON YOUR JOURNEY?
4. WHERE ARE YOU TRYING TO GO?
5. WHAT TOOLS DO YOU HAVE WITH YOU?
6. WHAT ARE YOUR BIGGEST CHALLENGES?

**30-MINUTE GET-LINKED-IN CALL PRE-WORK AND CALL OPENING**

**Directions:** Answer the questions below and use your answers as your introduction. After you introduce yourself, just listen. When the contact are done sharing his or her advice, you can move on to the additional call questions.

**1. THANK YOU & WHY YOU CHOSE THAT PERSON:**.................................................

..................................................................................................................................

..................................................................................................................................

**2. MY PURPOSE STATEMENT:**........................................................................................

..................................................................................................................................

..................................................................................................................................

**3. POINT A: WHERE AM I?**..............................................................................................

..................................................................................................................................

..................................................................................................................................

**4. POINT B: WHERE AM I TRYING TO GO?**...................................................................

..................................................................................................................................

..................................................................................................................................

**5. TOOLS I HAVE:**...........................................................................................................

..................................................................................................................................

..................................................................................................................................

**6. OBSTACLES I FACE:**.................................................................................................

..................................................................................................................................

..................................................................................................................................

## ADDITIONAL CALL QUESTIONS

If you're open to it, I have some additional questions written down that I would like to go through, otherwise you can just take what I've shared so far and give your advice. Perhaps you will answer a lot of my additional questions along the way.

### 1. GET ME RIGHT (ADVICE)
- Given skills and strengths I have, where do you think I can add the most value?
- Do you have any advice on the résumé I sent you and my positioning?
- Where do you see the company/industry going in five years?
- What's the biggest problem facing this company/industry right now?

### 2. GET ME ON (INFORMATION)
- Do you know of any listservs, websites, books, or blogs I should be up-to-date on?
- How do you stay so sharp? What are you reading every day?

### 3. GET ME OUT (NETWORKING)
- Are there any other events on your calendar that you think would be good for me so I could meet more people like you?
- If not, when great events come to you, would you e-mail them to me?

### 4. GET ME IN (LEADS)
- Do you have three friends, colleagues, or classmates in decision-making positions that you can recommend me to based on my qualifications?
- Do you know of any companies I should be on the lookout for?

### 5. GET ME UP (OPPORTUNITIES)
- Based on my value proposition, do you have opportunities that you think would be a fit for me?
- Do you know of any opportunities that would fit me?

# 3.5   HOW TO ENROLL YOUR FRIENDS IN YOUR CAREER DISCOVERY PROCESS

There are thousands and thousands of career paths to choose from, but for some reason, college students limit themselves to the big five—teacher, doctor, lawyer, engineer, accountant. Part of this is due to the fact that these are the primary professions that participate in on-campus recruiting.

However, when you take a step back and really look at the possibilities, there are three types of careers in the **Career Choice Circle**:

1. Careers you know exist and think you know a lot about.
2. Careers you've heard of but don't really know that much about.
3. Careers that you don't even know exist.

### Career Choice Circle

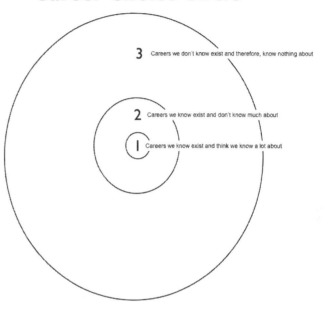

3   Careers we don't know exist and therefore, know nothing about

2   Careers we know exist and don't know much about

1   Careers we know exist and think we know a lot about

Our career choices are heavily influenced by our parents, peers, and professions we see on TV, when they should be driven by our passions and purpose. It's one thing to choose a career because your friends are doing it, but it's another thing to actually get your friends involved in your career discovery process by holding you accountable to your professional goals.

In this section, you will start a **30 Day Do It Group**, to help you create an accountability system around your professional goals. 30 Day Do It Groups meet once every 30 days and each person sets one career goal (e.g., finish the first draft of my resume, apply for three internships, do three informational interviews, find an alumni mentor and meet once). After 30 days, everyone reviews their goals, shares their progress, and sets a new goal. If you achieve your goal, you have to show proof, and you get celebrated by the group. If you don't achieve your goal, you have to pay the group with time, money, a physical activity, or something slightly embarrassing.

It's a fun way to keep you on track toward your career goals and ensure that you don't procrastinate in the midst of your academic rigor. Your career discovery process should start in your first year, not senior year. In fact, your career choice should come before you even choose a major because it is what should inform what major you choose. Your friends can help you get out of zone one of the Career Choice Circle and point out opportunities that you wouldn't have considered on your own.

## CAREER TEAM

**Directions:** Download the 30 Day Do It Group Starter Kit at http://www.innerviewing.me/30daydoit. List 2 people for each of the roles defined below. E-mail the pre-written invitation or use http://www.evite.com to send an invitation.

1. Builders are great motivators, always pushing you toward the finish line. They continually invest in your development and genuinely want you to succeed.

**My Builders:**.................................................................................................

2. A Companion is always there for you, whatever the circumstances. You share a bond that is virtually unbreakable.

**My Companions**:............................................................................................

3. Connectors are bridge-builders who help you to get what you want. They get to know you—and then connect you to others.

**My Connectors**:.............................................................................................

4. A Collaborator is a friend with similar interests—someone with whom you can easily relate. You might share a passion for sports, hobbies, religion, work, politics, foods, music, films, or books.

**My Collaborators**:...........................................................................................

5. Energizers are your fun friends, who always give you a boost. You have more positive moments when you are with these friends.

**My Energizers**:...............................................................................................

6. Mind Openers are the friends who expand your horizons with new ideas, opportunities, cultures, and people. They help you create positive change.

**My Mind Openers**:..........................................................................................

7. Navigators are the friends who give you advice, and keep you headed in the right direction. You go to them whenever you need guidance, and they talk through the "pros" and "cons" with you until you find an answer.

**My Navigators**:...............................................................................................

8. Champions stand up for you and what you believe in. They are loyal friends who sing your praises and defend you until the end.

**My Champions**:...............................................................................................

## INVITATION E-MAIL TEMPLATE

Edit and send the invitation below to all sixteen people above with the expectation that only six to ten will come. You can either send it as is using your regular e-mail account, or try a service such as Evite.com, Pingg.com, and Facebook Events. You can use www.30daydoit.com to help facilitate your goal tracking.

**SUBJECT:** Career Goal-Setting Party At My House, Wed. 7:00-8:30 p.m.

**BODY:** Hello Friends:

I have a renewed commitment to advancing my career. Ultimately, I want to invite you to join myself and others on this journey by having you come to a career goal-setting party at my house at 1000 Monument Way, New York, NY 11243 on Wednesday night from 7:00-8:30 p.m. People from a variety of industries also committed to professional development like you, will be there.

We're going to start at 7:00 p.m. sharp. Bring your career goals or any other goal written down. I will provide the goal-setting materials and some appetizers, but feel free to bring something if you would like. Please RSVP so that I can get a head count.

Cheers!

......................................................
YOUR NAME

## RECAP E-MAIL TEMPLATE

**SUBJECT:** Last Week's 30 Day Do It Recap

**BODY:** Hello, Goal Achievers:

Last week was amazing! I'm so inspired by each of you and your goals. Thank you for blessing my home.

**Our 30-Day Do It Goals are as follows:**

**Michelle:** Read us the first chapter of her book to create momentum toward her first book

**John:** Lose 10 pounds and squeeze into his old jeans so that he can be a better father to his athletic kids

**Jamie:** Clean her garage so that she can create a home office and show us before and after pictures

**Me:** Meet with 15 people for at least 15 minutes via phone or in person regarding my career change

The next 30 Day Do It will be at Mike's house on October 11th at 7:00 p.m. Bring a new member and snack if you can.

**When you get a chance:**
1. Take my "superhero" survey.
2. Forward me any job opportunities you come across.

Sincerely,

..................................................
       YOUR NAME

# 3.6 HOW TO FIND, ASK, & ENGAGE MENTORS

Mentors are more than a nice thing to have; they are essential if you want to accelerate your career. Mentors make the difference between people who simply advance up the corporate ladder one rung at a time and those who skip rungs.

Studies show that:
- Professionals who have used a mentor earn between $5,610-$22,450 more annually than those who don't. Among executives interviewed in one study, 75 percent say mentoring has played a key role in their careers.
- Those with mentors have higher job satisfaction, productivity, and retention.

Mentors are a key part of your network up. One powerful relationship up can equal the power of ten relationships across and a hundred relationships down. As a college student, great mentors can be any adult professional including your parents' friends, an alumni, a guest speaker who comes to campus, an old boss, a professor, or a staff member. You should respect their lifestyle and opinion and they should be willing to give you honest professional advice.

Once you identify a potential mentor, the next challenge is getting in contact with that person and building a sustainable relationship. The best way to get in contact is through someone whom you mutually know, or a formal mentor program offered by your school. What drives mentors is a desire to give back to someone who reminds them of themselves when they were younger, or someone who is doing things they wish they did. Ultimately, mentors want to help those following in their footsteps avoid some of the challenges they faced along their career paths that someone did or didn't prepare them for.

Even after a mentor commits, the next phase is keeping the mentor engaged after your first interaction. Like any relationship, good mentor-mentee relationships have structure. For example, you can establish a monthly meeting where one month is via phone and one month is in person. Otherwise, it can be a strictly phone and e-mail relationship if your mentor doesn't live in a nearby city.

In this section, you have all of the e-mail templates you need to reach out to your connections and potential mentors as well as a mentor meeting guide to structure your engagement and relationship. You have to lead the relationship and manage your mentor. Seek to give to your mentor as much as he or she gives to you and be prepared so that the mentor's time feels meaningful and respected.

**POTENTIAL MENTORS**

**Directions:** Identify three potential mentors and a contact and start e-mailing them.

**Example:**

A Potential Mentor's Name:..... *Dr. Smith*.................................
A. My Connection:.. *Mr. Edward Jones*...........................
B. Their Relationship To Each Other: *went to school together*............
C. Potential Mentor's Contact Information: *(345) 543-9854 or dr.smith@gmail.com*.....

**1. A Potential Mentor's Name:**.......................................

1A. My Connection:.................................................

1B. Their Relationship To Each Other:...............................

1C. Potential Mentor's Contact Information:..........................

........................................................................

**2. A Potential Mentor's Name:**.......................................

2A. My Connection:.................................................

2B. Their Relationship To Each Other:...............................

2C. Potential Mentor's Contact Information:..........................

........................................................................

**3. A Potential Mentor's Name**:.......................................

3A. My Connection:.................................................

3B. Their Relationship To Each Other:...............................

3C. Potential Mentor's Contact Information:..........................

........................................................................

## E-MAIL OR CALL TO MY CONNECTION

**SUBJECT:** Hi ....................................., Looking for your wisdom
               MY CONNECTION

**BODY:** Hi ...................................:
               MY CONNECTION

I hope all is well.

I need your help finding a mentor in the.........................................................................
                                                    INDUSTRY OR FIELD

I'm ready to accelerate my career, but I want proper guidance and direction, so I'm seeking to gain wisdom from people who are already where I want to be.

Can you think of any
• friends
• friends of friends
• classmates, or
• clients that you can connect me with?

...................................... came to mind. Do you think he would be a good person for me
    POTENTIAL MENTOR
to know, given my goals?

Flip through your cell phone numbers and see who pops up. If not, even ideas of where to look or go will help.

I appreciate your support.

Sincerely,

.................................................
        YOUR NAME

## E-MAIL OR CALL TO POTENTIAL MENTOR

**SUBJECT:** Hi ..................................., I was recommended by ....................................
POTENTIAL MENTOR                                              MY CONNECTION

**BODY:** Thank you ........................................,
MY CONNECTION

Hi ..........................................,
POTENTIAL MENTOR

My name is ...................................... and I've been seeking a mentor with experience in
YOUR NAME

.................................................................. I recently shared what I was looking for
INDUSTRY OR FIELD

with ...................................... and you were the first person that came to mind.
MY CONNECTION

I'm ready to accelerate my career, but I want proper guidance and direction, so I'm seeking to gain wisdom from people who are already where I want to be.

I'm currently ..................................................................................................
POINT A (COMPANY, COLLEGE, MAJOR)

but my goal is to ..............................................................................................
POINT B (CAREER ASPIRATION)

I would love to meet you via phone or in person. Please let me know when you have ten to fifteen minutes to talk.

Sincerely,

..............................................
YOUR NAME

## E-MAIL OR PHONE SCRIPT TO ASK MENTOR

Dear ...........................................................:

POTENTIAL MENTOR

## THANK YOU

First and foremost, I just want to thank you for your contribution to ................................

................................................................. through your amazing work on

INDUSTRY, FIELD, OR COMPANY

................................................................................................................

MAIN CONTRIBUTION OR AREA OF WORK

You are one of my pioneers and I'm excited to build a relationship with you.

## MY PURPOSE STATEMENT

I admire your journey from................................................ to now. I'm on a similar journey

LIFE STAGE WHERE YOU ARE (E.G., COLLEGE)

of my own and after some deep introspection, I've discovered that my passion is

................................................................................................................

................................................................................................................

## THE INVITATION

I know that in order to advance my career and make my greatest contribution to the

................................................................. like you have, I need guidance.

INDUSTRY, FIELD, OR COMPANY

I'm not sure if you have had mentors, or if you already have mentees today, but I would like to explore a mentoring relationship with you. I specifically need someone to occasionally call or e-mail on for factual and actionable advice. Please let me know if this is something you would be open to.

Thank you in advance,

..........................................

YOUR NAME

## 30 MINUTE MENTOR MEETING GUIDE

| | |
|---|---|
| Date, Time, & Phone | *August 1, 2010 at 5:00 p.m. at 243-534-8756* |
| Why this person? | *Rebecca has 15 years of experience in Human Resources* |
| Main Topic/Issue | *Career Advancement in Marketing* |
| Point A: Where am I? | *I am currently in college and about to graduate this Spring. I've done two internships with a focus in Human Resources thus far.* |
| Point B: Where am I trying to go? | *I am seeking an position in human resources at a mid-sized company in the technology sector. I have three target companies.* |
| Advance Questions | *- What should I be looking for in a great Human Resources manager?*<br>*- How do you see marketing being relevant to Human Resources?*<br>*- What are the companies with the highest retention rates of talent?*<br>*- Which company do you think would be best for me?* |
| New Questions | .................................................................<br>.................................................................<br>.................................................................<br>.................................................................<br>.................................................................<br>.................................................................<br>................................................................. |

| Notes/Advice | - It's not about the size, it's about your leadership and responsibility.<br>- Money is secondary to meaning, culture, and team<br>- Ask to do informational interviews.<br>- Look on LinkedIn to see if you know anyone there.<br>- You may want to position yourself as a recruiter instead of an HR executive given your marketing expertise.<br>- You should also consider head hunting firms instead of working for a single corporation. |
|---|---|
| Deliverables | Send Rebecca customized résumé and cover letter for each target company one week before next call |
| Next Meeting Date & Time | September 1, 2010 at 5:00 p.m. |

## 30 MINUTE MENTOR MEETING GUIDE

| | |
|---|---|
| Meeting Date, Time, & Phone | |
| Main Topic/Issue | |
| Point A: Where am I? | |
| Point B: Where am I trying to go? | |
| Advance Questions | |
| New Questions | |
| Notes/Advice | |
| Deliverables | |
| Next Meeting Date & Time | |

1. CREATE YOUR D.R.E.A.M. LIFE

2. ATTRACT YOUR D.R.E.A.M. CAREER

3. BUILD YOUR D.R.E.A.M. TEAM

**4.** **LAND YOUR D.R.E.A.M. JOB**

# 4.1 HOW TO GET AN INTERNSHIP OR FULL-TIME JOB

The greatest obstacle facing undergraduates when it comes to landing an internship is lack of work experience. Nowadays, even some internships require previous work experience, but how do you get work experience if you need work experience to get work? That's **the work experience trap** and the best way to overcome it is to create work for yourself by working for someone such as a professor or alumni for free, or for pay, on a project to which you commit to doing very well.

The big question that you need to answer to justify that you've done legitimate work is "What have you done that you are most proud of that has helped an individual or organization?" While considered great feats, getting into college, getting a 4.0, or even winning a scholarship aren't consider achievements that help others. That's what companies want. They want examples of things you have done that have created value for others since that's what they are in the business of doing.

You have a wide array of ways to create work experience for yourself including:
• On-campus jobs such as at the bookstore or as a residential advisor.
• Off-campus jobs such as a clothing store manager or tutor for high school students.
• Paid or unpaid research with a professor.
• A paid or unpaid internship in your desired field, or
• Entrepreneurship.

These kinds of experiences will prove that you are ready for the work world and, the more aligned your pre-internship experience is with your desired career path, the more likely it is that you will land the internship you want. For instance, if you want to work in media, you should work for the campus newspaper, radio station, and/or television station. Or if you want to work in marketing, seek a marketing role for the sports or admissions departments since marketing is a big part of their work.

A great internship is your ticket into your desired career path. According to a recent survey by the National Association of Colleges and Employers, employers will draw approximately 40 percent of their new college hires for 2011 from their internship and co-op programs. Furthermore, they expect to increase internships by about 7 percent in 2011 and co-op positions by nearly 9 percent. So, don't waste your summer or spring break doing nothing. The best way to get a job is to show that you can do the the job first.

Do a **Big Bang Project** on-campus or in your internship. Examples include finding a meaningful pro bono project to work on for a company that relates to your career or organizing a huge event. Don't settle for a filing and faxing job—find one that gives you responsibility and autonomy. The pre-internship job you create might not lead to an internship or full-time job from that company, but it will give you valuable work experience and relationships that you can leverage to open doors in the future.

**BIG BANG PROJECT**

**Directions:**
1. Visit the Career Center, Work-Study Office, a local company, or job boards to find an opportunity that interests you.
2. Identify three small problems in for the organization that you think are solvable and select the one that you think you can personally can have the most impact on.
3. Define the metrics that will let you know that you've positively impacted the problem.
4. Create an action plan to solve the problem in the allotted time.
5. Document your success with a short PowerPoint presentation and share it with the company before you leave.

**1. Identify 3 problems you see in your organization right now and the metrics associated with that specific problem.**

**Example:**
Problem: Customer Dissatisfaction
Metrics: Retention, Repeat Customers, Revenues


❐ **Problem 1:**....................................................................................................................

Metrics:.............................................................................................................................


❐ **Problem 2**:...................................................................................................................

Metrics:.............................................................................................................................


❐ **Problem 3:**..................................................................................................................

Metrics:.............................................................................................................................


**2. Put a checkmark next to the problem above that you think you can make the most impact on in the time you have left.**


**3. You will know that you positively impacted the problem when you have...**

..........................................................................................................................................

and the metric moves from.............................................to...............................................

**4. Create an action plan to solve the problem.**

| X | ACTION ITEM | DUE DATE |
|---|---|---|
| | | |
| | | |
| | | |
| | | |
| | | |
| | | |
| | | |
| | | |

**5. After you've successfully completed the project, document your results in an off-boarding presentation to the organization.**

**SLIDE 1 TITLE: Cover Page**
- Company logo
- Name
- Presentation Title
- Date

**SLIDE 2 TITLE: My Top 3-5 Goals (in coming here)**
- One ultimate goal
- 3-5 sub-goals

**SLIDE 3 TITLE: My Updated Résumé**
- 10 new Point A to Point B bullet points using the 13Cs

**SLIDE 4 TITLE: My High Moments and Low Moments**
- 5-8 high moments
- 3-5 low moments

**SLIDE 5 TITLE: Special Thank Yous**
- Include everyone in some way
- Be specific about what you're thankful for (e.g., Nicole: for your trust and creative freedom)

**SLIDE 6 TITLE: My Wish List**
- Have fun, but also be serious
- For the CEO
- For your manager
- For your team
- For the secretary (i.e., a staple gun to shoot people who steal her stapler)
- For the IT guy
- For other people and departments
- For the company as a whole

**SLIDE 7 TITLE: My Next Steps**
- Your new company
- Your new title
- Your new responsibilities

**SLIDE 8 TITLE: My Contact Information**
- Name
- E-mail
- LinkedIn
- Phone (Optional)

# 4.2 HOW TO USE THE INTERNET TO FACILITATE YOUR JOB SEARCH

According to Nielsen Online, in January 2009, at the height of the financial crisis, there were 49.7 million unique visitors to job board sites, up from 41.5 million unique visitors in January 2008, an increase of 20 percent. CareerBuilder Network was the top destination with 20.8 million visitors, followed by Yahoo! HotJobs, and Monster, with 11.7 million and 9.5 million unique visitors, respectively. Some other statistics worth noting include:

- Major Job boards boast a measly 1 to 4 percent average response rate. That's a lot of résumés to send out just to hear nothing back!
- Online résumé posting yields only an 8 percent chance of success of uncovering the next opportunity (4 percent from employers and 4 percent from recruiters)
- 46 percent of successful job seekers made a direct application to the employer. (26 percent applied online, 10 percent to hiring manager, and 10 percent to Human Resources department)
- 45 percent of your leads will come from using the Internet as your lead generator—8 percent résumé posting, 31 percent online published openings, 6 percent e-mail/online networking

The Internet is a research tool more than a recruiting tool. Once you research a particular posting and company, it's up to you to find and build relationships with real people through e-mail, phone, and networking. A lot of people apply for jobs online and feel productive after uploading dozens of résumés, but without the other real touches, résumés get lost in a black hole that doesn't return invitations to interview.

In addition to the major job boards, there are a lot of niche or industry-specific job boards where your results may increase because your application is more targeted. For instance, you can go to Idealist.org for nonprofit jobs, InternQueen.com for internships, or a site like Dice.com for technology jobs. Outside of job boards, you can also use Google to target your searches with search operators, Google Alerts to create a **Job "Perch" Engine**, and Craigslist. You also have your Career Center, Work Study Office, and job boards on campus that may have job opportunities that align with your career goals.

Always keep in mind that job boards are one place to search for jobs, but job opportunities are everywhere (that a problem exists), so don't limit yourself to online searches and applications. You're also searching for people in addition to postings because, according to the Wall Street Journal, 90 percent of jobs are filled through employee referrals. Facebook.com and LinkedIn.com have more accurate searchable data about your friends and network than you can remember, and great jobs aren't always listed, so use the people you know to get what you want.

## GOOGLE BASIC SEARCH OPERATORS

**Directions:** Test out these Google search operators to explore how you can use Google.com to get more relevant search results.

| OPERATOR EXAMPLE | FINDS PAGES CONTAINING... |
| --- | --- |
| consulting jobs | the words consulting and jobs |
| consulting OR consultant | either the word consulting or the word consultant |
| "is now hiring" | the exact phrase "is now hiring" |
| jobs −recession | the word jobs but NOT the word recession |
| +career | only the word career, and not the plural or any tenses or synonyms |
| ~teaching jobs | jobs info for both the word teaching and its synonyms: professor, instructor, and so forth |
| define:computer | definitions of the word computer from around the Web |
| red * blue | the words red and blue separated by one or more words |
| I'm Feeling Lucky | takes you directly to first web page returned for your query |
| facilitate site: www.idealist.org | the words "facilitate" ONLY within www.idealist.org |
| related: www.mckinsey.com | similar content as www.mckinsey.com (which is essentially their competitors/counterparts) |

## USING GOOGLE TO FIND LOCAL JOBS

1. Go to http://www.google.com.
2. Type in "[JOB/FUNCTION]" and "City" e.g., "mechanical engineer Oakland" (542,000 results).
3. Put quotations around mechanical engineer --> "mechanical engineer" Oakland (207,000 results).
4. Click "advanced search" and click "Date, usage rights, numeric range, and more."
5. Change "Date" to "past week" (49,000 results).
6. Change "Date" to "past 24 hours" (12,000 results).

## USING GOOGLE TO FIND NEW JOB OPENINGS

1. Go to http://www.google.com.
2. Type in "[JOB/FUNCTION] jobs" e.g., "consulting jobs" and hit search.
3. On the left, click "More" and then click "Updates."
4. Review the Twitter, Facebook, and FriendFeed for opportunities.

## USING GOOGLE TO FIND A NICHE & POSITION YOURSELF

1. Go to http://www.google.com.
2. Type in [JOB/FUNCTION] and hit search.
3. On the left, click "More search tools."
4. Click "Wonder Wheel."
5. Click on the link that says [JOB/FUNCTION] jobs.
6. Continue to do this and observe the other related niche job titles that branch out.

## USING GOOGLE TO SEE WHERE YOUR PROFESSION HAS BEEN AND WHERE IT IS GOING

1. Go to http://www.google.com.
2. Type in [JOB/FUNCTION] and hit search.
3. On the left, click "More search tools."
4. Click "Timeline."
5. Click the right side of the timeline bar graph after 2000.
6. Click on "2010."
7. Look for trends, company names, interesting news, and opportunities.

## CREATE YOUR DAILY JOB "PERCH" ENGINE

**1. Choose 6 search terms that you want Google to inform you about daily.**

**Examples:** "Consulting jobs," "McKinsey"

1.............................................. 4..............................................

2.............................................. 5..............................................

3.............................................. 6..............................................

**2. Go to http://www.google.com/alerts and enter your search terms and preview your results.**

**TARGET COMPANIES**

**Examples:** "McKinsey" OR "Deloitte" OR "BCG" OR "Booz"

**TARGET POSITIONS**

**Examples:** "consulting jobs" OR "marketing jobs" OR "sales jobs"

**Examples:** "looking for consultants" OR "looking for marketers"

**Examples:** "hiring teachers" OR "looking for teachers"

**OTHER KEY PHRASES**

**Examples:** "job openings" OR "looking for qualified candidates" OR "looking for qualified applicants" OR "send your résumé" OR "now hiring" OR "job opportunities" OR "looking to expand" OR "new market" OR "merges with" OR "fastest growing"

**3. Select how frequently you want to receive the alerts via e-mail and then click "Create Alert."**

## RESEARCHING COMPANIES & JOBS

**LINKEDIN.COM**

**Find the companies where you know people & how many job openings they have**
1. Go to http://www.linkedin.com/companies?trk=tab_compy.
2. Narrow your search by industry, location, country, postal code, company size.

**Search your target companies & find the people you are closest to**
1. Go to http://www.linkedin.com/companies?trk=hb_tab_compy.
2. Type in one of the names of your target companies.
3. Click "Follow company."
4. Click the same link that now says "Stop following" to edit the "Notification Settings" to get notified when job opportunities are posted.

**Now that LInkedln is working for you, change your notification settings**
1. Go to https://www.linkedin.com/settings/?tab=email.
2. Change your settings to immediately or weekly based on the urgency of your career change.

**FACEBOOK.COM**

**Find the companies where you know people**
1. Go to your profile.
2. Click on "Friends" under your profile picture.
3. At the top of the page, click on the menu that says "Search by Name" and go down to "Search by Workplace."
4. Type in the name of the company you are considering working at.
5. Go to their profile, grab their e-mail address, and send them a professional e-mail expressing your interest in their company with a link to your website and your résumé attached.

**Check friends' status updates**
1. Go to http://www.facebook.com/search.
2. In the search box on the left, type "hiring" and hit search.
3. Scroll down to the bottom of the page and click "View All Post By Friends."

**TWITTER.COM**

### Find opportunities without registering for anything

1. Go to http://twitter.com/search?q#search?q=%23jobs OR http://twitter.com/search?q#search?q=%23job.
2. Scan the jobs that are listed.
3. Do multiple searches using each of your keywords from the Google Alerts module.
4. For more advanced searches, go to http://search.twitter.com/advanced.

### Find opportunities using http://tweetajob.com

1. Go to http://www.twitter.com and create an account if you don't already have one.
2. Go to http://tweetajob.com/jintro.
3. Login with your Twitter account by clicking the "Sign in with Twitter" button.
4. Click the "Allow" button. You will be redirected back to http://tweetajob.com.
5. Update your profile at http://tweetajob.com/jeditprofile and click "Save."
6. Go to http://tweetajob.com/jeditcategory and select your job categories and click "Save."
7. Click on "My Jobs" (http://tweetajob.com/jprofile) to see all the listings relevant to you.
8. Scroll down to the map on the right and add any other cities you are willing to work in.

For more information on how to use Twitter to search for jobs, download this FREE ebook: http://twitterjobsearchebook.files.wordpress.com/2010/02/tweetajob_updfeb10_ebook.pdf.

# HOW TO PROPERLY RESEARCH A CAREER PATH FOR FIT

Your **career fit** is the alignment between who you truly are, and who an organization or industry needs you to be. In the interviewing process, there are four versions of who you are at the table:

1. Who you truly are.
2. Who you think you need to be.
3. Who the potential employer thinks you are.
4. Who the employer truly needs you to be.

The perfect career fit is when who you truly are is who they truly need you to be.

The best way to ensure that you find a career that is a fit is to narrow down your infinite choices with the **Career Cone**.

**CAREER CONE**

**1. Purpose:** We examined your purpose through the innerview process from Module 1, and you want to keep that at the forefront of any career decision. Your purpose is unique to you because only you have the unique combination of passions, problems, and people that you care about.

**2. Profession:** Given your purpose, what professions would allow you to live it every day? This answer may be a general industry or career category such as engineering, social work, education, or finance. There are many ways to fulfill your purpose, but which professions seem like the best fit?

**3. Path:** From here you want to get more specific and determine the specific type of path you want to pursue within the industry or field. For instance, there are all types of engineers: architectural, civic, computer, electrical, industrial, mechanical, and transportation, among others. Choose which one you think is the best fit for you.

**4. Position:** Finally, you want to start looking for positions or postings that match the career path that you are seeking. We will explore how to measure a company for fit in the next section, but now that you know what you want, you should learn more about the position (e.g., average day, salary, trends, requirements, etc.) and identify the job boards, associations, and pioneers in this space.

The career cone will help you narrow down your unlimited career options to a career that is aligned with your purpose, so that you can have a fulfilling fitting career.

## HOW TO MEASURE YOUR FIT

**Fit:** Refer back to your 30 second pitch in Module 1.13 and use yours to evaluate how closely a career and a company match it.

**Problems It Solves:** Get problems or questions that this career path solves on a daily basis by asking people who work(ed) on that career path.

**Top Three Daily Actions:** Get the top three verbs from asking people who work/ed on the career path what they do during their typical work day.

**People I Know:** Conduct searches on Facebook and LinkedIn to identify with similar career paths or job titles as the one you have chosen.

**Pioneers:** Do a Google search for "pioneer in [FUNCTION]." e.g., "pioneer in consulting." Focus on finding individuals whose career paths you can learn from and model. If you find a company, look at the life of its founder.

**Job Boards:** Go to the list of 400+ job boards at http://www.innerviewing.me/job-search-engines or do a Google search for "[INDUSTRY/FUNCTION] jobs" (e.g., "consulting jobs") and look for sites in the first page of results.

**Associations:** Do a Google search for "[INDUSTRY/FUNCTION] association" (e.g., "education association" or "teaching association") and look through the first page of results.

**Salary Range:** Go to http://www.payscale.com/index/US/Job, http://www.salary.com or http://www.glassdoor.com.

**Current Trends:** Go to http://biz.yahoo.com/ic/ind_index.html and find your industry to see how it's doing financially. Go to http://www.prnewswire.com/search/advanced and search industry to see the latest mentions about your industry.

**Types/Niches:** Do a Google search for "types of [FUNCTION]" (e.g., "types of engineers").

**Applied Industries:** Go to http://www.payscale.com/index/US/Job, find your job title, and scroll to industries.

**Barriers To Entry and Requirements:** These barriers should be outlined in the job description or posting. Common barriers include education, exams, and experience.

**Prospective Companies:** Go to http://www.vault.com/wps/portal/usa/companies and find your industry or function. If it's not there, do a Google search for "best [FUNCTION] companies" or "top [FUNCTION] companies" (e.g., "top life coaching companies").

## CAREER FIT

**Directions:** Complete the following worksheet to evaluate whether your chosen career path is a fit for you.

**Career Path:**.................................................................................................................

**Fit**
This career path aligns with my personal....

❐ Principles ❐ Passions ❐ Problems ❐ People ❐ Positioning ❐ Pioneers ❐ Picture ❐ Possibility

**Research**

Problems It Solves:...........................................................................................................

Top Three Daily Actions:...................................................................................................

People I Know:..................................................................................................................

Pioneers:.........................................................................................................................

Job Boards:......................................................................................................................

Associations:....................................................................................................................

Salary Range:...................................................................................................................

Current Trends:.................................................................................................................

Types/Niches:...................................................................................................................

Applied Industries:............................................................................................................

**Barriers To Entry & Requirements**

Education:.......................................................... Years of Experience:..................

Certificates/Licenses:.......................................................................................................

Other:..............................................................................................................................

**Prospective Companies**

................................................................     ................................................................

................................................................     ................................................................

# 4.4  HOW TO PROPERLY RESEARCH A COMPANY SO YOU INTERVIEW AS FEW TIMES AS POSSIBLE

Recruiting is not about the number of interviews you get. It's about how close the job you land is to your actual D.R.E.A.M. job. The most successful recruiting season would be where an individual finds their D.R.E.A.M. job, courts the company, interviews with only them, and lands the job. When you have too many interviews, especially in a variety of industries or functions, it shows lack of self-awareness and spreads you thin.

Once you find the industry and function you want to work in using the career cone, the next step is finding a company. It's possible to land your D.R.E.A.M. job in a nightmare company. All companies are not the same, and one size does not fit all. Companies are distinct in a variety of ways such as the following:

**Size:** In some cases, bigger is better, but not every case. Perhaps a start-up environment is better for your career than a big-name brand because it means more responsibility and opportunities for growth.

**Location:** Do you want to live in an apartment in an urban environment, or a four-bedroom house in a rural neighborhood? How long a commute to work will you accept? Can you telecommute? Would you telecommute? Are you willing to work in a foreign country? It may seem insignificant, but location can be a deal breaker.

**Culture:** Some companies are quiet and some are noisy. Some have cubicles and others have open spaces. Some require suits and others don't. Some are competitive and some are collaborative. You have to think about what type of work environment you thrive in and find a company that creates those conditions.

**Work-Life Balance:** Are you willing to work 80 hours per week and weekends when necessary, or do you want to stop at 40 or 50 hours, no matter what? Do you think health care and child care should be covered? What if you have to travel two times per week? These are things you have to consider as you choose a prospective employer.

**Mission:** Do you want to work for a company where the only focus is money, or do you want to make meaning and money? There are for-profit companies that do meaningful work, and there are nonprofits that are focused only on raising more money. You have to decide if work means more than just making money to you.

**Other:** Is diversity important to you, or are you okay with working in a homogeneous environment? Is it okay if you're a woman and there are no women executives? How would high turnover or cold layoffs affect you?

What looks good on paper, may not be good in real life. The interview process is about you getting to know the company just as much as it is them getting to know you. Don't accept a job offer—even if it's your only one—unless it feels like a fit

**COMPANY FIT**

**Directions:** Conduct in depth research on a company, job, and culture of one of your target employers using the the 8 Cylinders of Success framework to find a fit.

**Example Company:**...*Apple*.................................................................

**Job Title:**..*iTunes Store Product Marketing Manager*.......................................

**The Company** (from company website and "About Us" page)

| | 8 CYLINDERS OF SUCCESS | FIT? |
|---|---|---|
| Principles | This company believes:<br>*innovation, easy of use, revolutionary* | X |
| Passions | This company is passionate about:<br>*creating cool technology products* | X |
| Problem | This company solves the problem of:<br>*how to create tools that help people create what they want* | X |
| People | This company's target market includes:<br>*Cultural Creatives* | X |
| Positioning | This company wants to be the best at:<br>*world's leading technology & innovation company* | X |
| Pioneers | This company's pioneers and competitors include:<br>*Microsoft* | X |
| Picture | This company's vision is:<br>*a world where people are free to create* | X |
| Possibility | This company makes it possible for:<br>*a world with no unrealized ideas* | X |

**COMPANY FIT**

**Company:**.................................................................................

**Job Title:**.................................................................................

**The Company** (from company website and "About Us" page)

| | 8 CYLINDERS OF SUCCESS | FIT? |
|---|---|---|
| Principles | This company believes: | |
| Passions | This company is passionate about: | |
| Problem | This company solves the problem of: | |
| People | This company's target market includes: | |
| Positioning | This company wants to be the best at: | |
| Pioneers | This company's pioneers and competitors include: | |
| Picture | This company's vision is: | |
| Possibility | This company makes it possible for: | |
| Purpose | It's stated purpose or mission is: | |

**POSITION FIT**

**The Job** (from job description & posting)

| | 8 CYLINDERS OF SUCCESS | FIT? |
|---|---|---|
| Principles | This job was created based on the belief in/that:<br>*ease of use, nice design* | *x* |
| Passions | This job requires passion for:<br>*working with UI, software engineering, working with media* | *x* |
| Problem | This job was created to solve the problem of:<br>*how to expand the use of iTunes with existing and new customers* | *x* |
| People | This job serves the following external/internal customers:<br>*media consumers (music, videos, books, etc.)* | *x* |
| Positioning | This job requires expertise in/at:<br>*multi-media distribution center* | *x* |
| Pioneers | The world's best at this job include:<br>*none* | *x* |
| Picture | The vision for this job is to:<br>*create a one-stop shop for every form of digital media* | *x* |
| Possibility | This job makes it possible for the company/customers to:<br>*listen, watch, & experience what you want instantly* | *x* |
| Purpose | The primary purpose of this job is:<br>*to create a shopping experience that helps people find and buy media* | *x* |

**POSITION FIT**

**The Job** (from job description & posting)

| | 8 CYLINDERS OF SUCCESS | FIT? |
|---|---|---|
| Principles | This job was created based on the belief in/that: | |
| Passions | This job requires passion for: | |
| Problem | This job was created to solve the problem of: | |
| People | This job serves the following external/internal customers: | |
| Positioning | This job requires expertise in/at: | |
| Pioneers | The world's best at this job include: | |
| Picture | The vision for this job is to: | |
| Possibility | This job makes it possible for the company/customers to: | |
| Purpose | The primary purpose of this job is: | |

**COMPANY CULTURE**

| | NOTES | GRADE |
|---|---|---|
| Company | Go to http://www.glassdoor.com.<br><br>**NOTES:** | |
| Industry | Go to http://biz.yahoo.com/ic/ind_index.html.<br><br>**NOTES:** | |
| Stocks | Go to http://finance.yahoo.com.<br><br>**NOTES:** | |
| Press | Go to http://www.prnewswire.com/search/advanced and search the industry and company.<br><br>**NOTES:** | |
| News | Go to http://news.google.com.<br><br>**NOTES:** | |
| Interviews | Go to http://www.vault.com, type in company and read "Reviews" or go to http://www.glassdoor.com, type in company and click "Interviews."<br><br>**NOTES:** | |

**THE LIFESTYLE**

| | LIFESTYLE NOTES | GRADE |
|---|---|---|
| Ex. Work/Life Balance | *60 hours/week, some weekends, seasonal stress* | *B+* |
| Work/Life Balance | | |
| City and Commute | | |
| Salary and Bonus | | |
| Benefits and Vacation | | |
| Leadership/ Mgrs. | | |
| Products/ Services | | |
| Teammates | | |
| Growth Opportunity | | |
| Feedback/ Mentor | | |

# 4.5 HOW TO IDENTIFY THE PROBLEM THE COMPANY IS HIRING YOU TO SOLVE

Every job a company posts is connected to some problem internally or externally that is preventing the Average Business Cycle from spinning as fast as it can. In the same way that a business that's not solving a problem or creating an outcome for the customer will actually go out of business, a job that is no longer relevant to the business model won't exist for long.

All kinds of clues about the problem a company needs solved, and for which it is hiring a problem-solver, can be found in the job description it posts. The more you focus on the problem and potential solutions to help them overcome that problem in your cover letter and interview and demonstrate how you've solved similar problems in the past through your résumé, the more likely it is that you will get the job.

The notion that "there are no jobs" is completely false because every business has problems or inefficiencies that can be improved. There are no perfect businesses out there. The question is "Are you the best person to solve the problem a company has? Further, will the problem you solve create more value for the company than it takes to pay you?"

In many respects, even an employee must have an entrepreneurial spirit. **Intrapreneur** is a term used to describe someone who moves within a company like an entrepreneur moves through the world. An intrapreneur is always looking for meaningful problems to solve that can improve the company environment. Any jobs or employees that function like a machine will be replaced by one eventually, or the jobs will be outsourced to other countries where labor is cheaper.

Therefore, rather than waiting to be told what to do by a manager, the twenty-first century employee will look for things to do that can't be automated, outsourced, or solved by a computer alone. The person who indicates that he or she can best solve the unique problem the job was created to solve, using examples from his or her past performance, will be a front runner in the hiring process.

Review the **13 Cs of Résumé Bullet Writing (See Module 2.8)** and explore whether the problems defined in the job description fit in one of those buckets, and then identify experiences you've had that show that you have solved similar problems. This is how you make your strongest case for the given position.

**SAMPLE JOB DESCRIPTION**

**Position:**
Direct Marketing Coordinator

**Description**:
The Direct Marketing Coordinator will work with our product, marketing and sales teams to support marketing initiatives.

**Responsibilities:**
- Prepare and execute weekly voice shot marketing campaigns.
- Import and manipulate data and materials as needed for each campaign.
- Vendor/interface management.
- Communicate with field/centers to coordinate local events for support.
- Conduct monthly reporting of activity.
- Work with Copywriter, Art, and Brand Managers to strategize scripts.
- Coordinate special projects.
- P/L responsibilities: manage costs/budget.

**Example**

**Problems:** *Customer reach, data-driven decision making, budgeting, innovation*

**Problem 1:** *Customer reach*

My Experience: *During my time at INC, I successfully executed texting and phone campaigns to reach the same target market that ACME serves, thus condensing our recruiting season by half.*

**Problem 2:** *Data-driven decision-making*

My Experience: *At INC, I created an extensive Microsoft Access database to effectively track weekly numbers, which were used to guide weekly planning and accountability measures.*

## JOB DESCRIPTION READING

**Directions:** Find a job description for one of your target companies. Read through the job description and look for the top four problems that job was created to solve. List them below and then briefly share an experience you've had solving a similar problem.

**Company:**................................................ **Job Title:**...........................................................

**Problem 1:**...............................................................................................................

My Experience:.............................................................................................................

..................................................................................................................................

..................................................................................................................................

**Problem 2:**...............................................................................................................

My Experience:.............................................................................................................

..................................................................................................................................

..................................................................................................................................

**Problem 3:**...............................................................................................................

My Experience:.............................................................................................................

..................................................................................................................................

..................................................................................................................................

**Problem 4:**...............................................................................................................

My Experience:.............................................................................................................

..................................................................................................................................

..................................................................................................................................

# 4.6 HOW TO ANSWER THE TOP 10 INTERVIEW QUESTIONS WITH CONFIDENCE

When you've properly innerviewed, your answers to the top ten interview questions will come naturally. A great interviewer's goal is simply to get the stories behind your application to evaluate your past performance. While it's a great thing to let your personality shine, an interviewer is really there to learn more about your past performance to evaluate if you can do the job the company needs done.

When writing your résumé, you learned the Point A to Point B résumé bullet format. That same format applies for your interview answers. Each résumé bullet has a story behind it that speaks to who you are, and you will use that structure to tell a more elaborate story about what happened and how you got the results you did. To refresh your memory from Module 2, the Point A to Point B résumé bullet works like this:

**Point A to Point B Résumé Bullet Example**

| | |
|---:|---|
| VERB: | Pioneered |
| WHAT: | a Go Green Save Green recycling program |
| POINT A: | decreasing our waste |
| POINT B: | by half |
| ACTION: | by leveraging video conferencing for regional meetings |

Given the bullet above, questions that you can delve into to help elaborate on your résumé bullet during your interview with a story could include:
• What made you pioneer this initiative? What was everyone else doing?
• Why did you create this program?
• How did you notice the waste and measure your results?
• How effective were the video conferences?
• What technology did you use?

Your answer to these questions will paint a more vivid picture of what was happening when you arrived, and then what happened as result of your thoughtful actions. This format also applies the STAR Method for answering questions. The STAR Method works as follows:

S – Situation, background set the scene.
T – Task or Target, specifics of what's required, when, where, who.
A – Action, what you did, skills used, behaviors, characteristics.
R – Result – Outcome, what happened.

Successful interviewing has just as much to do with listening as it does with talking. A key thing to listen for is the question behind the question. When an interviewer asks a question, listen carefully, and look for what kind of information they are trying to get at and then give it to them with a thorough answer that addresses all of the follow questions you can anticipate. Answering their unasked questions, will set you apart.

**QUESTION 1: So, tell me a little about yourself.**

**The questions behind the question:**
The interviewer really wants a cursory overview of who you are and why you're here.
Some sub-questions that you should answer, but may not be explicit include:
• Why did you apply for the position?
• What relevant experience do you have?
• What's your educational background?
• How did you find out about us?

**Key Points:**
• Give them your **30 Second Pitch (See Module 1.13)** in a conversational manner.
• Mention general things on your resume about your school, major, employment, and leadership.
• Highlight skills directly relevant to the position you are applying for.

**My Answer:**

..............................................................................................................................

..............................................................................................................................

..............................................................................................................................

..............................................................................................................................

..............................................................................................................................

..............................................................................................................................

..............................................................................................................................

..............................................................................................................................

..............................................................................................................................

..............................................................................................................................

..............................................................................................................................

..............................................................................................................................

..............................................................................................................................

..............................................................................................................................

**QUESTION 2. Why do you want to work at this company?**

**The questions behind the question:**
The interviewer really wants to know what you know about their company and why you think you're a fit for the position. Some sub-questions that you should answer, but may not be explicit include:
• Why have you chosen this field of work?
• What do you know about our business? Our products? Our services?
• What do you know about our industry?
• How does your major connect to our work?
• What other companies and careers have you considered?

**Key Points:**
• Share what you know about the company's business model using the **Average Business Cycle (See Module 2.11)** template from memory.
• State your top 5 strengths **(See Module 1.16)** from the Gallup *StrengthsFinder 2.0* and then highlight how your unique combination supports their business model and fits the position.
• Include any inside information you learned about the company, competition, or industry to show that you've done your research.
• Mention the name of a mentor or someone you know in the industry or the company to show that you know what you're getting into.

**My Answer:**

..........................................................................................................................

..........................................................................................................................

..........................................................................................................................

..........................................................................................................................

..........................................................................................................................

..........................................................................................................................

..........................................................................................................................

..........................................................................................................................

..........................................................................................................................

..........................................................................................................................

**QUESTION 3. What relevant experience do you have?**

**The questions behind the question:**
The interviewer really wants to know if you've done similar work in the past. Some sub-questions that you should answer, but may not be explicit include:
- Do you understand the day-to-day work of someone in this field?
- Even if you've never worked in this field, do you have any transferable experiences that can give me insight to the results you might be able to create here?
- Will you be able to jump right in and go or will we have to hold your hand and train you?

**Key Points:**
- Cite two examples or stories you have from your **transferable skills (See Module 1.15)** related to problems listed in the job description.
- Show them something from your **Résumé 2.0** or portfolio **(See Module 2.11)** if you have anything that proves your ability to do the work.

**My Answer:**

........................................................................................................................................

........................................................................................................................................

........................................................................................................................................

........................................................................................................................................

........................................................................................................................................

........................................................................................................................................

........................................................................................................................................

........................................................................................................................................

........................................................................................................................................

........................................................................................................................................

........................................................................................................................................

........................................................................................................................................

........................................................................................................................................

**QUESTION 4. If your friends, classmates, or professors were here, what would they say about you?**

**The questions behind the question:**
The interviewer really wants to know how honestly you see yourself. Some sub-questions that you should answer, but may not be explicit include:
- Are you likable?
- Are you a team player?
- How well do you communicate with others?
- Are you able to self-evaluate and self-correct?

**Key Points:**
- Pull two or three adjectives from your eulogy **(See Module 1.11)** since it was written from the perspective of your best friend.
- State the adjectives up front and then offer stories that support why someone would say that about you.
- If you have an actual example that you can cite of someone affirming you, use it.

**My Answer:**

..........................................................................................................................

..........................................................................................................................

..........................................................................................................................

..........................................................................................................................

..........................................................................................................................

..........................................................................................................................

..........................................................................................................................

..........................................................................................................................

..........................................................................................................................

..........................................................................................................................

..........................................................................................................................

..........................................................................................................................

..........................................................................................................................

**QUESTION 5. Have you done anything to further your experience?**

**The questions behind the question:**
The interviewer really wants to know what you've done to distinguish yourself that is above and beyond what the average candidate brings to the table. Some sub-questions that you should answer, but may not be explicit include:

- What classes did you take specifically in preparation for this career that you didn't have to take?
- Do you do any reading related to this work? Are there any books, magazines, or websites you read regularly?
- What type of events have you engaged in relevant to this work? Any conferences, networking events, or seminars that the average applicant may not have participated in?

**Key Points:**
- Mention studying the lives of pioneers in the field **(See Module 1.10)** or certain relevant topics with your professors and mentors.
- Mention books, magazines, and blogs you read as well as one's you've written **(See Module 3.3)**.
- Mention any relevant classes, conferences, and certificates.

**My Answer:**

..................................................................................................................................

..................................................................................................................................

..................................................................................................................................

..................................................................................................................................

..................................................................................................................................

..................................................................................................................................

..................................................................................................................................

..................................................................................................................................

..................................................................................................................................

..................................................................................................................................

..................................................................................................................................

## QUESTION 6. What motivates you to do a good job?

**The questions behind the question:**
The interviewer really wants to know what drives you to succeed. Some sub-questions that you should answer, but may not be explicit include:
- What motivates you? Money? Recognition? Competition? Growth? Fear? Friends? Parents? Failure? Impact?
- Will you succeed in our organization given how it is set up?
- Are you intrinsically motivated (e.g., self-starter, intrapreneur) or do you need extrinsic motivators (e.g., money, titles, awards)?
- What will you aim for when you can't measure your success with a GPA?

**Key Points:**
- Share a story about something you achieved that you are extremely proud of and then draw out the people, emotions, and things that motivated you to achieve that goal.
- Give an example of a non-academic project or a goal that you initiated achieved simply because you wanted to do it such as your **Big Bang Project (See Module 4.1)**.

**My Answer:**

.................................................................................................................................

.................................................................................................................................

.................................................................................................................................

.................................................................................................................................

.................................................................................................................................

.................................................................................................................................

.................................................................................................................................

.................................................................................................................................

.................................................................................................................................

.................................................................................................................................

.................................................................................................................................

.................................................................................................................................

**QUESTION 7. What's your greatest strength?**

**The questions behind the question:**
The interviewer really wants to know how you think you added the most value to things you've been involved with. Some sub-questions that you should answer, but may not be explicit include:
- Do you know what makes you unique?
- Is your greatest strength relevant to our work?
- If so, how will your strength make you a top performer in this position?

**Key Points:**
- Pull from the Gallup *StrengthsFinder 2.0* (**See Module 1.16**). Choose your strength with the most powerful example and tell the Point A to Point B story.
- Connect your strength and story to the position and company's business model by explaining how you think it will make you great at the job.
- Show something from your **Résumé 2.0 (See Module 2.11)** or portfolio that demonstrates your strength and supports your story.

**My Answer:**

.......................................................................................................................................

.......................................................................................................................................

.......................................................................................................................................

.......................................................................................................................................

.......................................................................................................................................

.......................................................................................................................................

.......................................................................................................................................

.......................................................................................................................................

.......................................................................................................................................

.......................................................................................................................................

.......................................................................................................................................

.......................................................................................................................................

.......................................................................................................................................

.......................................................................................................................................

**QUESTION 8. What's your biggest weakness?**

**The questions behind the question:**
The interviewer really wants to know if you have any red flags that would prevent you from being able to do the work. Some sub-questions that you should answer, but may not be explicit include:
• Is there anything I should be aware of that you aren't telling me?
• I know you've put your best foot forward for the interview, but what's the real truth about your performance and personality?
• How do you handle difficult questions and moments like this one?

**Key Points:**
• Give an example of a time when you've overused a strength **(See Module 1.16)** and it actually hurt you (e.g., "My initiative sometimes manifest as impatience.").
• State what you've done to proactively limit the overuse of your strength in a certain area (e.g., coaching, a ritual, etc).
• Conclude by mentioning some area for growth such as developing non-critical technical skills that you know you will be trained in if you get the job, but aren't expected to know coming in (e.g., using Salesforce, selling financial derivatives, etc).

**My Answer:**

..............................................................................................................................

..............................................................................................................................

..............................................................................................................................

..............................................................................................................................

..............................................................................................................................

..............................................................................................................................

..............................................................................................................................

..............................................................................................................................

..............................................................................................................................

..............................................................................................................................

..............................................................................................................................

..............................................................................................................................

**QUESTION 9. So, explain why I should hire you.**

**The questions behind the question:**
The interviewer really wants to know how serious you are about this career path and pursuing it with their company. Some sub-questions that you should answer, but may not be explicit include:
• Why this company...again?
• Given all the career paths out there, why this one?
• Why this particular position?
• If I take a risk and invest in you, how long are you going to stay?

**Key Points:**
• Mention the top 3 reasons you like this company in comparison to it's competitors to show that you've done your research **(See Module 4.4)**.
• Cite how yours and their **8 Cylinders of Success (See Module 4.4)** align.
• State why and how you chose this career path and why you are committed to succeeding in it.
• Reiterate why your strengths, skills, and story make you the perfect fit for this position.

**My Answer:**

..............................................................................................................................

..............................................................................................................................

..............................................................................................................................

..............................................................................................................................

..............................................................................................................................

..............................................................................................................................

..............................................................................................................................

..............................................................................................................................

..............................................................................................................................

..............................................................................................................................

..............................................................................................................................

..............................................................................................................................

**QUESTION 10. Finally, do you have any questions to ask me?**

**The questions behind the question:**
The interviewer really wants to know how thorough and direct you are. An interview is an opportunity for you to get to know an employer just as much as it is an opportunity for them to get to know you. Some sub-questions that you should answer, but may not be explicit include:
- How thoughtful are your questions? Could you have found the answer on your own elsewhere?
- If you have questions, will you ask them or do you refrain from asking questions because you're afraid of looking like you don't know something?
- Do you seek clarity or brush over important details?
- Do you see me as a professional peer that you can talk with eye-to-eye or as an adult not to be questioned?

**Key Points:**
- Use your questions as an opportunity to show what know by prefacing them with background information first and then asking the question?
- Never ask something that you could have found on your own elsewhere.
- Make sure your questions are sincere. Don't ask a question just to ask.

**Examples:**
- What has been your most rewarding/significant project or experience working here?
- Sometimes job descriptions don't tell all, so in your own words, how would you define the problem that this position was created to solve?
- How does this position fit into the overall business model of the organization?
- How will my success be measured?
- Assuming I advance in the interview process, what would be the next steps?
- When should I expect to hear back from you?

**My Answer:**

................................................................................................................

................................................................................................................

................................................................................................................

................................................................................................................

................................................................................................................

................................................................................................................

................................................................................................................

# 4.7 HOW TO KEEP A POTENTIAL EMPLOYER ENGAGED AFTER THE INTERVIEW

Similar to the challenge of engaging mentors after an initial interaction, there is a challenge engaging potential employers after an interview. Hiring decisions aren't usually made right after your interview, so you have to keep the lines of communication open until they hire someone—hopefully, you. In fact, only 18 percent of Fortune 100 companies send e-mails when the position is full. So you have to creatively stay on the company's radar until the employer makes a hiring decision without annoying anyone to a point where the company doesn't want you around.

Three things need to occur within 48 hours of the interview: a thank you e-mail, a thank you card, and a self overview.

**Thank You E-mails:** The purpose of the thank you e-mail is straightforward—it's to say thank you. The thank you e-mail shows that you are grateful for the interviewer's time and the opportunity, and that you are still interested. It is possible that you may not be interested after the interview once you do your overview and assess how you feel about the company, but you should still send a thank you e-mail to keep the door open. Thank you e-mails should be sent separately to each person who interviewed you and have some customization that speaks specifically to them so that it feels authentic and not pasted from a template.

**Thank You Card:** A thank you card has to do with your level of professionalism more so than it does with saying thank you. It communicates your follow through, and that you are sincere and serious about this opportunity. This act alone can set you apart. Whereas anyone can send a follow up e-mail in minutes, a hand-written thank you card takes time and money, even if it is not that much money. In addition, a thank you card serves as a physical reminder of you as the interviewers weigh their options. Either send one card to the decision maker or send a card to each interviewer. It's safer to do the latter because you may not know who the final decision maker is, and you don't want anyone to feel slighted or insignificant over saving a few dollars to buy and send a card.

**Your Overview:** The interview is your greatest opportunity to learn about the company beyond the website. In addition to how you feel and what occurs in the interview, you can also observe other information like how welcoming people are, how excited they are to be there, how the office is designed, people's workspaces, and what all that may say about the organization. The website can tell you only so much, so it's important to assess how you feel about the company and position after you get this new information to see if you still feel like the opportunity is a fit for you.

## INTERVIEW FOLLOW UP

**Directions:** After every interview, capture the following information for your interviewer and use it when sending them a thank you card and e-mail.

**Interview Name 1:**..................................................................................................

Position:................................................ E-mail:..............................................

This person's response to your significant/rewarding project or experience question:

..................................................................................................................

One interesting thing you remember about this person (e.g., I ride a bike to work daily.):

..................................................................................................................

❏ Thank you e-mail sent    ❏ Thank you card mailed

**Interview Name 2:**..................................................................................................

Position:................................................ E-mail:..............................................

This person's response to your significant/rewarding project or experience question:

..................................................................................................................

One interesting thing you remember about this person (e.g., I'm from California.):

..................................................................................................................

❏ Thank you e-mail sent    ❏ Thank you card mailed

**Interview Name 3:**..................................................................................................

Position:................................................ E-mail:..............................................

This person's response to your significant/rewarding project or experience question:

..................................................................................................................

One interesting thing you remember about this person (e.g., I have a 2 year old son.):

..................................................................................................................

❏ Thank you e-mail sent    ❏ Thank you card mailed

## THANK YOU E-MAIL TEMPLATE

Dear..........................................,
       INTERVIEWER'S NAME

I just want to say thank you for the opportunity to interview with you yesterday.

I appreciate your time, your insights on the organizational culture, and your daily contribution to the company's mission.

I'm excited about the possibility of working with you and bringing the value I have to

offer to.................................................. as the new .........................................................
       COMPANY NAME                                POSITION/JOB TITLE

After my visit, I'm convinced that there is a fit. Your experience working with/on

.....................................................................................................................................
       SIGNIFICANT PROJECT MENTIONED IN THE INTERVIEW

characterizes the types of experiences I want to have in my professional career.

I look forward to hearing from the hiring committee within the next week. Until then, I invite you to visit my professional website and blog at www.yourname.com to see my extended résumé and a recent article I wrote related to the future of our industry.

Sincerely,

.................................................
       YOUR NAME

**THANK YOU CARD TEMPLATE**

Dear............................................,
            INTERVIEWER'S NAME

I know that I already expressed my gratitude via e-mail, but sometimes efficiency doesn't equal effectiveness, especially when it comes to communication within organizations. Sometimes you have to go the extra mile.

I'm grateful to have advanced to this stage of the interview process, and I am glad to have heard your unique perspective on your experience here. I definitely believe that this is a place where I can create value, I will be valued, and I can express my values.

Thanks again!

Sincerely,

.................................................
            YOUR NAME

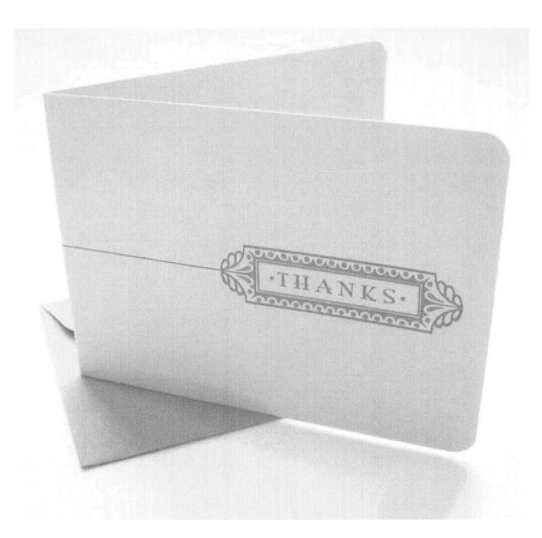

## OVERVIEW OF THE INTERVIEW

**Directions:** Copy and complete this worksheet after every interview you have to capture new information about the position, and how you can improve next time.

Company:................................Position:...............................................

What did I learn about myself? (Not for me, I build good rapport, a little nervous, etc.)

..........................................................................................................

..........................................................................................................

..........................................................................................................

What did I learn about the position? (qualities I seek, problem it solves, metrics, etc.)

..........................................................................................................

..........................................................................................................

..........................................................................................................

What did I learn about the company? (nobody was smiling, very quiet, etc.)

..........................................................................................................

..........................................................................................................

What areas do I need to do more research or study in before future interviews?

..........................................................................................................

What question/s stumped me?.......................................................................

..........................................................................................................

When should I expect to hear back?...............................................................

If necessary, how can I prepare better for my next interview?...........................

..........................................................................................................

..........................................................................................................

..........................................................................................................

# 4.8 HOW TO CREATE A POWERFUL 3 MONTH INTERNSHIP PLAN & MANAGE YOUR BOSS

Earlier you wrote your retirement speech as if it were the last day your amazing career because you were officially retiring. Now, imagine that you are going to leave the company where you currently work in three to five years. What do you want your aspirational résumé to look like when you leave? If you determine this in advance, and let your manager know, your likelihood of achieving your aspirations will increase significantly.

In addition to your aspirational résumé, you should set personal, intellectual, social, and financial capital goals for your new job.
* How do you want to challenge yourself? Perhaps by working abroad?
* What new skills or subjects do you want to master? Public speaking? Financial planning?
* How do you want to expand your network? New mentors?
* What are your salary and savings goals by the time you leave?

Determining these things up front will help you know when you have outgrown your job, and it's time to move forward internally or externally.

Your manager is going to be your greatest ally in achieving your career vision. Whether the manager is fully aware, partially aware, or unaware of your goals, he or she will be your pipeline for projects, reservoir for relationships, and input for information. The more the manager is aware of your goals, the more he or she can intentionally help you. Some of your goals may be better off kept to yourself, so use your good judgment based on your relationship with your manager.

Although your boss manages you, you have to manage the boss's expectations. Regular, scheduled communication with your boss outside of regular meetings will relieve you of any surprises when it comes to your performance evaluation. It's important that you and your boss agree up front on how your success will be measured. Early success on something meaningful that may be beyond your job description can give you instant credibility and put you on the fast track to success internally. You can create another **Big Bang Project** for your employer on an important business problem over which you have autonomy and can show measurable results. Showing your undeniable value immediately is the key to your long-term success.

Managing up is a skill. In the same way your manager manages down to get what he or she wants from you, you have to manage up to get what you want from the manager and the company. Relationship patterns tend to get established quickly, but you can shape the trajectory of your relationship and experience with a series of self-initiated meetings early on that help you and your manager get on the same page. As a result, you can both have the happy ending you desire from working together.

## MY FIRST 90 DAYS

**Directions:** Imagine that this is just a bridge job you are planning to maximize and transition from in 18 months or less. Answer the questions below with this mindset.

### Personal Capital
What are four ways I can use this position to develop my personal capital?
(e.g., take on uncomfortable/challenging projects, ask for feedback, strengths testing, etc.)

1..............................................................................................................................

..............................................................................................................................

2..............................................................................................................................

..............................................................................................................................

3..............................................................................................................................

..............................................................................................................................

4..............................................................................................................................

..............................................................................................................................

### Intellectual Capital
What are four ways I can use this position to develop my intellectual capital?
(e.g., paid training, conferences, three skills I want to develop, foreign language, etc.)

1..............................................................................................................................

..............................................................................................................................

2..............................................................................................................................

..............................................................................................................................

3..............................................................................................................................

..............................................................................................................................

4..............................................................................................................................

..............................................................................................................................

**Social Capital**

What are four ways I can use this position to develop my social capital?
(e.g., mentors, board of directors, networking events, etc.)

1..............................................................................................................................

..............................................................................................................................

2..............................................................................................................................

..............................................................................................................................

3..............................................................................................................................

..............................................................................................................................

4..............................................................................................................................

..............................................................................................................................

**Financial Capital**

What are four ways I can use this position to develop my financial capital?
(e.g., set a savings goal, try to get a full-time offer, practice by doing private
consultations, etc.)

1..............................................................................................................................

..............................................................................................................................

2..............................................................................................................................

..............................................................................................................................

3..............................................................................................................................

..............................................................................................................................

4..............................................................................................................................

..............................................................................................................................

## OFF-BOARDING SPEECH

**Directions:** Write your retirement speech as if you were going to work at this company for ten years. Use elements from your original speech, but make it specific to the company you work for now. Be sure to include:

• Awesome projects and products that you worked on;
• Real or fictitious people who you helped or who helped you along the way;
• Your super hero name; and
• Results, results, results that impacted the company, customers, or colleagues.


........ years and ......... months from today, ..............., ........, 20.........

...........................................................................................................................

...........................................................................................................................

...........................................................................................................................

...........................................................................................................................

...........................................................................................................................

...........................................................................................................................

...........................................................................................................................

...........................................................................................................................

...........................................................................................................................

...........................................................................................................................

...........................................................................................................................

...........................................................................................................................

...........................................................................................................................

...........................................................................................................................

...........................................................................................................................

**NEW RÉSUMÉ BULLETS**

**Directions:** Envision that you are at the end of your time at your current company. Write 1-2 résumé bullet points for each of the 13Cs of Résumé Bullet Writing that you would like to have on your resume by the time you move on.

**1. Customer or Consumer:** Write 1-2 bullet points about how you moved a metric related to customers from Point A to Point B (e.g., loyalty, satisfaction, dollars per purchase, net promoter score, etc.).

....................................................................................................................................

....................................................................................................................................

....................................................................................................................................

....................................................................................................................................

**2. Cash Flow:** Write 1-2 bullet points about how you moved a metric related to cash flow from Point A to Point B (e.g., increased inflow, decreased outflow, etc.).

....................................................................................................................................

....................................................................................................................................

....................................................................................................................................

....................................................................................................................................

**3. Company:** Write 1-2 bullet points about how you moved a metric related to the company from Point A to Point B (e.g., rankings in best places to work, # of new clients, labor standards, decrease percent of defective products & returns, etc.).

....................................................................................................................................

....................................................................................................................................

....................................................................................................................................

....................................................................................................................................

**4. Colleagues:** Write 1-2 bullet points about how you moved a metric related to your colleagues from Point A to Point B (e.g., retention increase, on-board time decrease, grew full-time-equivalents (FTE) increase, number of mentorship relationships established, number of 360-degree feedback sessions completed, increased percent who participated in company retreat, increase in job security, etc.).

........................................................................................................................

........................................................................................................................

........................................................................................................................

........................................................................................................................

**5. Community:** Write 1-2 bullet points about how you moved a metric related to the community from Point A to Point B (e.g., number of hours volunteered, amount of matching funds, number of mentorships, dollar amounts of pro bono work, etc.).

........................................................................................................................

........................................................................................................................

........................................................................................................................

........................................................................................................................

**6. Capital:** Write 1-2 bullet points about how you moved a metric related to the capital from Point A to Point B (e.g., increase in assets, decrease in debt, mergers, acquisitions, division sold, financing raised, etc.).

........................................................................................................................

........................................................................................................................

........................................................................................................................

........................................................................................................................

**7. Culture:** Write 1-2 bullet points about how you moved a metric related to the company culture from Point A to Point B (e.g., increased employee satisfaction, number of innovative projects, employee safety rating, etc.).

........................................................................................................................

........................................................................................................................

........................................................................................................................

**8. Campaign:** Write 1-2 bullet points about how you moved a metric related to an internal or external campaign from Point A to Point B (e.g., page views, conversion rate, media impressions, subscribers, etc.).

..................................................................................................................

..................................................................................................................

..................................................................................................................

..................................................................................................................

**9. Champion of Change:** Write 1-2 bullet points about how you moved a metric related to a change you led from Point A to Point B (e.g., carbon emissions decrease, switched software & executed national training, shifted market from computers to consulting, etc.).

..................................................................................................................

..................................................................................................................

..................................................................................................................

..................................................................................................................

**10. Communication:** Write 1-2 bullet points about how you moved a metric related to the company communication from Point A to Point B (e.g., integrated a CMS, established meeting process and protocol, created a Wiki to share intelligence, etc.).

..................................................................................................................

..................................................................................................................

..................................................................................................................

..................................................................................................................

**11. Competition:** Write 1-2 bullet points about how you moved a metric related to the competition from Point A to Point B (e.g., passed Toyota for #1 spot, increased market share by 10%, competition closed 5 stores in new market, etc.).

..................................................................................................................

..................................................................................................................

..................................................................................................................

..................................................................................................................

**12. Collaboration:** Write 1-2 bullet points about how you moved a metric related to collaboration or partnerships from Point A to Point B (e.g., built new supplier relationship, landed $100K sponsorship, led cross-divisional team to create new product, etc.).

......................................................................................................

......................................................................................................

......................................................................................................

......................................................................................................

**13. Concepts:** Write 1-2 bullet points about how you moved a metric related to concepts you created from Point A to Point B (e.g., created a new business line that grew to $4M, revamped lead generation process using my 4Ps framework, etc.).

......................................................................................................

......................................................................................................

......................................................................................................

......................................................................................................

**MEETING #1: INTERVIEW YOUR BOSS**

**Our Company's Purpose**

In your own words, why does our company exist?

.......................................................................................................................

.......................................................................................................................

What is your vision for this company or, more specifically, our division?

.......................................................................................................................

.......................................................................................................................

How is your company or division's success measured? What are the metrics?

.......................................................................................................................

.......................................................................................................................

**Your Position's Purpose**

In your eyes, what is the purpose of your position?

.......................................................................................................................

.......................................................................................................................

What should I come/look to you for?

.......................................................................................................................

.......................................................................................................................

**My Position's Purpose**

In your eyes, what is the purpose of my position?

.......................................................................................................................

.......................................................................................................................

How will my success be measured by you? What are the metrics I should be aware of?

........................................................................................................................

........................................................................................................................

## My On-Boarding Process

Do you have any strategic documents that you can share with me so I can learn more about where we are and where we're trying to go?

How is each team member/division on the organization chart critical to our success?

Are there any readings that shaped your view of our company, customer, or positions?

Do you mind if we have a 30-minute one-on-one check-in meetings every 30 days?

## Other Notes:

........................................................................................................................

........................................................................................................................

........................................................................................................................

........................................................................................................................

........................................................................................................................

........................................................................................................................

........................................................................................................................

........................................................................................................................

........................................................................................................................

........................................................................................................................

........................................................................................................................

**MEETING #2: DASHBOARD, OFF-BOARDING SPEECH, & RÉSUMÉ**

### Dashboard

1. Based on the metrics of success given during the last meeting and what you've observed with the company culture, create a dashboard for yourself.
2. Share the dashboard with your manager and ask him or her if he or she agrees with the metrics you've chosen and how you're measuring them.

### Off-Boarding Speech

1. Share the speech with your boss so that he or she can have a clear vision of your vision.

### Future Résumé

1. Share your ten-year bullet points with your boss as well.
2. Request ideas and feedback on how to make your vision a reality.

# END

## THE APPENDIX

MY TO-DO LIST
MY RESEARCH
MY CHOICES
MY RESOURCES

## MY TO-DO LIST

- ☐ .........................................................................................................................................
- ☐ .........................................................................................................................................
- ☐ .........................................................................................................................................
- ☐ .........................................................................................................................................
- ☐ .........................................................................................................................................
- ☐ .........................................................................................................................................
- ☐ .........................................................................................................................................
- ☐ .........................................................................................................................................
- ☐ .........................................................................................................................................
- ☐ .........................................................................................................................................
- ☐ .........................................................................................................................................
- ☐ .........................................................................................................................................
- ☐ .........................................................................................................................................
- ☐ .........................................................................................................................................
- ☐ .........................................................................................................................................
- ☐ .........................................................................................................................................
- ☐ .........................................................................................................................................
- ☐ .........................................................................................................................................
- ☐ .........................................................................................................................................
- ☐ .........................................................................................................................................
- ☐ .........................................................................................................................................

## NEW PEOPLE TO EXPLORE

☐.........................................................    ☐.........................................................

☐.........................................................    ☐.........................................................

☐.........................................................    ☐.........................................................

## NEW INDUSTRIES TO EXPLORE

☐.........................................................    ☐.........................................................

☐.........................................................    ☐.........................................................

☐.........................................................    ☐.........................................................

## NEW CAREER PATHS TO EXPLORE

☐.........................................................    ☐.........................................................

☐.........................................................    ☐.........................................................

☐.........................................................    ☐.........................................................

## NEW SKILLS TO EXPLORE

☐.........................................................    ☐.........................................................

☐.........................................................    ☐.........................................................

☐.........................................................    ☐.........................................................

## NEW NEWS TO EXPLORE

☐.........................................................    ☐.........................................................

☐.........................................................    ☐.........................................................

☐.........................................................    ☐.........................................................

## NEW PROBLEMS & OPPORTUNITIES TO EXPLORE

☐ ................................................
☐ ................................................

☐ ................................................
☐ ................................................

☐ ................................................
☐ ................................................

## NEW COMPANIES TO EXPLORE

☐ ................................................
☐ ................................................

☐ ................................................
☐ ................................................

☐ ................................................
☐ ................................................

## NEW WEBSITES TO EXPLORE

☐ ................................................
☐ ................................................

☐ ................................................
☐ ................................................

☐ ................................................
☐ ................................................

## NEW BOOKS TO EXPLORE

☐ ................................................
☐ ................................................

☐ ................................................
☐ ................................................

☐ ................................................
☐ ................................................

## NEW TRENDS TO EXPLORE

☐ ................................................
☐ ................................................

☐ ................................................
☐ ................................................

☐ ................................................
☐ ................................................

## NEW VOCABULARY WORDS TO EXPLORE

☐....................................................   ☐....................................................

☐....................................................   ☐....................................................

☐....................................................   ☐....................................................

## NEW EVENTS TO EXPLORE

☐....................................................   ☐....................................................

☐....................................................   ☐....................................................

☐....................................................   ☐....................................................

## NEW ORGANIZATIONS & ASSOCIATIONS TO EXPLORE

☐....................................................   ☐....................................................

☐....................................................   ☐....................................................

☐....................................................   ☐....................................................

## OTHER THINGS TO EXPLORE

☐....................................................   ☐....................................................

☐....................................................   ☐....................................................

☐....................................................   ☐....................................................

☐....................................................   ☐....................................................

☐....................................................

☐....................................................

☐....................................................

☐....................................................

☐....................................................

**NEW CHOICES & DECISIONS I'M MAKING REGARDING MY CAREER**

..................................................................................................

..................................................................................................

..................................................................................................

..................................................................................................

..................................................................................................

..................................................................................................

**THINGS I'M STILL INDECISIVE ABOUT BUT COMMIT TO RESEARCHING**

..................................................................................................

..................................................................................................

..................................................................................................

..................................................................................................

..................................................................................................

..................................................................................................

**ASSUMPTIONS I HAVE, BUT WANT TO CHALLENGE ABOUT MY CAREER**

..................................................................................................

..................................................................................................

..................................................................................................

..................................................................................................

..................................................................................................

..................................................................................................

**Company Research**
http://finance.yahoo.com
http://www.glassdoor.com/index.htm
http://www.hoovers.com
http://investing.businessweek.com
http://sec.gov/edgar.shtml
http://www.vault.com
http://www.zoominfo.com

**Rankings**
http://www.greatplacetowork.com
http://money.cnn.com/magazines/fortune/bestcompanies

**Networking**
http://www.brazencareerist.com
http://www.identified.com
http://www.linkedin.com
http://www.springboardr.com

**Career Paths**
http://www.linkedin.com/careerexplorer/dashboard
http://www.onetonline.org
http://www.oneweekjob.com
http://www.payscale.com/gigzig.aspx

**Salary**
http://www.payscale.com
http://www.salary.com/mysalary.asp

**General Job Boards**
http://www.careerbuilder.com
http://www.hotjobs.com
http://www.monster.com

**Internships**
http://www.internqueen.com
http://www.internships.com
http://www.internshipprograms.com
http://www.internzoo.com
http://www.summerinternships.com

**Non-Profit**
http://www.cgcareers.org
http://www.idealist.org
http://www.guidestar.org

**Volunteering**
http://www.catchafire.com

**Website Builder**
http://www.about.me
http://www.beyondcredentials.com
http://www.weebly.com
http://www.wix.com
http://www.wordpress.com

**Assessments**
http://www.keirsey.com
http://www.myersbriggs.org
http://www.strengthsfinder.com/home.aspx

**Other Websites**
http://www.careeralism.com
http://www.careerrocketeer.com
http://www.quintcareers.com
http://www.personalbrandingblog.com

**Books**
-101 Things To Do Before You Graduate by Patricia Hudak & Jullien Gordon
-Career Renegade by Jonathan Fields
-Dig This Gig by Laura Dodd
-Do More Great Work by Michael Bungay Stainer, Seth Godin, Michael Port, & Dave Ulrich
-Do What You Are by Paul D. Tieger & Barbara Barron
-Linchpin by Seth Godin
-Never Eat Alone by Keith Ferrazzi
-Now What? by Nicholas Lore
-Pathfinder by Nicholas Lore
-Rework by Jason Fried & David Heinemeier Hansson
-StrengthsFinder 2.0 by Tom Rath
-Success Built To Last by Jerry Porras, Stewart Emery, & Mark Thompson
-What Color Is Your Parachute? by Richard Nelson Bolles
-Work On Purpose by Laua Galinsky & Kelly Nuxoll
-The Wow Factor by Frances Cole Jones